Contents

1. **Introduction**...1
   Background and Purpose of the Forum 1
   Organization of This Report 4

2. **Background on Arab, South Asian, Muslim, and Sikh Communities in the United States**...........5
   Arabs...5
   South Asians...6
   Muslims 7
   Sikhs 8

3. **Understanding Islam in America in the Aftermath of September 11**...................................9
   Yahya Hendi, Muslim Chaplain, Georgetown University, and Imam, Islamic Society
       of Frederick, Maryland...9
   Sanaulla Kirmani, Adjunct Professor of Philosophy and Religion, Goucher College....................11
   Yvonne Haddad, Center for Muslim-Christian Understanding, Georgetown University.............12
   Nedzib Sacirbey, Interim Director, American Muslim Council 13
   Clark Lobenstine, Executive Director, InterFaith Conference of Metropolitan Washington........13

4. **National Crises, Civil Rights, and Civil Liberties: A Historical Review**.......................15
   Kit Gage, Director, First Amendment Foundation and National Committee
       Against Repressive Legislation 15
   James X. Dempsey, Deputy Director, Center for Democracy and Technology 16

5. **Implementing the USA Patriot Act of 2001: Civil Rights Impact**...................................19
   Laura W. Murphy, Director, Washington Office, American Civil Liberties Union 20
   Malea Kiblan, Immigration Attorney, Kiblan & Battles...21
   Kelli M. Evans, Civil Rights Attorney, Rehlman Associates 22
   Raj Purohit, Legislative Counsel, Washington Office, Lawyers Committee for Human Rights ...23
   Paul K. Martin, Counselor, Office of the Inspector General, and Acting Special Counsel
       for Civil Rights/Civil Liberties, Department of Justice 24
   Blane Workie, Trial Attorney, Office of Aviation Enforcement and Proceedings,
       Office of the General Counsel, Department of Transportation 25
   Kathleen A. Connon, National External Program Manager, Office of Civil Rights,
       Federal Aviation Administration, Department of Transportation...................................26

6. **Fears and Concerns of Affected, At-Risk Communities** 27
   Johari Abdul-Malik, Muslim Chaplain, Howard University 30
   Kareem W. Shora, Legal Advisor, American-Arab Anti-Discrimination Committee 30
   Rajwant Singh, President, Sikh Council on Religion and Education.....................................32
   Sharifa Alkhateeb, President, North American Council for Muslim Women 33
   Gautam Dutta, Vice President, South Asian Bar Association 34
   Joseph Zogby, Special Counsel for Post-September 11 National Origin Discrimination,
       Civil Rights Division, Department of Justice 35

7. **Local Government Responses and Best Practices** 36

    Ronald Clarkson, Community Relations Manager, Office of the County Executive,
        Montgomery County, Maryland.. 36

    Charles Moose, Chief of Police, Montgomery County, Maryland 37

    James Ashton, Virginia Department of Education (representing Dr. Jo Lynne DeMary,
        State Superintendent of Public Instruction, Virginia Department of Education) 38

    Brian Boykins, Assistant District Commander, Mason District, Fairfax County Police, Virginia .. 38

    Penelope Gross, Member of the Board of Directors, Metropolitan Washington Council of
        Governments, and Mason District Supervisor, Fairfax County, Virginia 38

    Sharee Freeman, Director, Community Relations Service, Department of Justice 39

    Susan Douglas, Principal Researcher, Council on Islamic Education 39

    Jason Erb Government Relations Officer, Council on American-Islamic Relations 40

8. **Key Observations Based on Forum Testimony** 41

Appendices

1. Dissenting Statement by Stephen Kurzman, DC SAC Member... 45
2. Editorial Committee's Clarifications to the Dissenting Statement by Stephen Kurzman 47

Chapter 1

Introduction

On April 24 and 25, 2002, the District of Columbia, Maryland, and Virginia Advisory Committees to the U.S. Commission on Civil Rights held a joint community forum focusing on civil rights concerns in the Washington, D.C., metropolitan area in the aftermath of the September 11, 2001, terrorist attacks. The two-day public forum at the Mason District Government Center in Annandale, Virginia, included presentations by representatives of affected population groups, specifically Arabs, South Asians, Muslims, and Sikhs; federal, state, and local government agencies; legal and advocacy organizations; and community groups. This report summarizes the presentations made by panelists during the forum and includes brief observations by the Advisory Committees based on the testimony and limited additional research.

Background and Purpose of the Forum

The attacks against the World Trade Center and the Pentagon on September 11, 2001, by terrorists from Middle Eastern countries led to a dramatic surge in hate violence and discrimination against people in the United States perceived to be of Arab or Muslim background, most of whom are either U.S. citizens or legal residents.[1] Within hours of the hijackings, even as prominent Arab American and Muslim American organizations were issuing statements condemning the terrorist attacks, the backlash began.[2] There were two hate-related murders, of an Indian Sikh and a Pakistani Muslim, on September 15, and another murder of an Asian Indian on October 4. Over the following weeks and months, civil rights advocacy organizations, media, and local and federal law enforcement agencies around the country received reports of attempted murder, physical assaults, death threats, and hate speech against individuals, as well as vandalism, arson, shootings, and threats against homes, businesses, and places of worship. There were also persistent reports of discrimination, especially in air travel and in the workplace. The victims of these incidents included a wide array of people—Arabs and Muslims but also South Asians, including Sikhs, and even other individuals such as Latinos mistakenly perceived to be members of these groups.[3]

The day after the hijackings, on September 12, 2001, the U.S. Commission on Civil Rights issued a statement conveying its deepest sympathies to the victims of the heinous terrorist attacks and warning that Americans should not compound the tragedy through expressions of

---

[1] Hate violence and discrimination against Arab Americans are not new, and the U.S. Commission on Civil Rights has a history of concern about these issues. In September 1999, the Michigan Advisory Committee held a public forum on civil rights issues facing the large Arab American community in that state, leading to publication of a report based on the situation in Michigan but of nationwide relevance. Issues included profiling of Arab Americans at airports, denial of due process in deportation hearings, and discrimination in employment, religious, and educational spheres. *See* Michigan Advisory Committee to the U.S. Commission on Civil Rights, *Civil Rights Issues Facing Arab Americans in Michigan,* May 2001. Unless otherwise noted, statements and reports of the Commission and its Advisory Committees are available on the Commission's Web site at <www.usccr.gov>.

[2] *See* Arab American Institute, "Arab American Statement on Terror Attacks," Sept. 11, 2001, and "Joint Arab-American, Muslim-American Statement," Sept. 12, 2001, <www.aaiusa.org/aai_statement.htm> (Oct. 27, 2002).

[3] The surge in hate crimes and discrimination against these groups in 2001 has been documented by the Federal Bureau of Investigation and by the American-Arab Anti-Discrimination Committee as well as other advocacy groups. *See* the summary of Panel Four.

religious or ethnic intolerance.[4] This was followed by a statement in which the Commission noted the troubling rise in reported bias incidents and urged tolerance, saying:

> As our nation pursues the criminals who committed these acts, we must not allow our desire to find those responsible lead us to irresponsible and un-American behavior. We must not compromise any person's civil rights or civil liberties. No one should be a target simply because they are, or appear to be, a member of a particular ethnic or religious community.[5]

The Commission established a toll-free telephone hot line to receive calls from individuals who believed they had been victims of civil rights abuses as part of the post-September 11 backlash. After hundreds of complaints were received the first week, the Commission established a second hot line to accommodate the volume of calls.[6] Information received over the hot lines has helped the Commission to identify affected communities and gauge the frequency, nature, and geographic distribution of discrimination incidents and hate crimes.[7]

At the same time, concern was also growing among civil liberties advocates over implications of the new national policies and laws enacted or proposed as part of the federal government's nationwide response to terrorism. On October 12, 2001, the Commission held a public briefing on U.S. immigration policies, practices, and laws in the aftermath of the terrorist attacks.[8] Representatives of the Immigration and Naturalization Service (INS) and the U.S. Department of Transportation (DOT) as well as community organizations and legal experts discussed racial profiling in air travel, bias in immigration procedures, and the government's detention of thousands of Middle Eastern men in the aftermath of September 11.

Immediately after the September attacks, the Commission urged its State Advisory Committees (SACs) to take a proactive role in bringing community and government leaders together to tackle civil rights issues raised by September 11 and its aftermath. The SACs responded with forums, briefings, and meetings with local community groups and leaders, which have taken place in 20 states and territories across the country.[9] As part of this effort, the Commission's Eastern Regional Office formed an Inter-SAC Committee drawn from the District of Columbia, Maryland, and Virginia Advisory Committees in order to bring a joint perspective to issues in the national capital area, which spans the three jurisdictions. Members and staff believed that a collaborative effort, rather than parallel efforts by the three individual SACs, could achieve a more comprehensive and in-depth examination of issues in the metropolitan area.

In working on post-September 11 civil rights concerns, the Washington, D.C., metropolitan area was considered of particular importance for several reasons. First, the Virginia and Maryland suburbs of Washington are home to large populations of people of Middle Eastern and South Asian origin. Indeed, the metropolitan Washington area is one of the top five urban areas with the largest populations of Arab Americans and is also among the top five areas for Asian Indian Americans, the most numerous of the South Asian groups in this country. Virginia and Maryland are both among the top 10 states in the nation in the size of their Muslim popula-

---

[4] U.S. Commission on Civil Rights, "Statement of the U.S. Commission on Civil Rights," press release, Sept. 12, 2001.

[5] U.S. Commission on Civil Rights, "U.S. Commission on Civil Rights Announces Complaint Line to Protect Rights of Arab, Islamic Communities; Urges Tolerance in the Face of Tragedy," press release, Sept. 14, 2001.

[6] U.S. Commission on Civil Rights, "U.S. Commission on Civil Rights Launches Second Complaint Hotline to Accommodate Great Response: Charges of Vandalism to Personal Property and Harassment by Neighbors, Employers Dominate Calls," press release, Sept. 19, 2001.

[7] By September 2002, the Commission had responded to approximately 597 telephone complaints and 50 written complaints related to September 11. Approximately 258 complaints were referred to federal agencies, principally the Department of Justice and the Equal Employment Opportunity Commission. Most complaints involved employment discrimination, harassment by neighbors and the general public, harassment in school, harassment by police and immigration officers, airline discrimination, and property damage. See U.S. Commission on Civil Rights, "Anniversary Update on Commission Activities Related to September 11," September 2002.

[8] U.S. Commission on Civil Rights, "Briefing on Boundaries of Justice: Immigration Policies Post-September 11," Oct. 12, 2001.

[9] For a detailed description of these SAC activities, see U.S. Commission on Civil Rights, "Anniversary Update on Commission Activities Related to September 11." Of particular note, the Commission convened its July 2002 meeting in Detroit to learn firsthand from its Midwestern State Advisory Committees about the post-September 11 civil rights problems facing Arab Americans and Muslims in their states.

tions; Muslims in the local area include not only people of immigrant backgrounds but also many African American Muslims. All these groups have a vibrant organizational presence in Washington and its suburbs, with mosques, community centers, Islamic schools, and other ethnic and religious organizations.

Second, Northern Virginia was the site of the terrorist attack on the Pentagon, and the national capital area is thus one of the parts of the country most directly affected by the events of September 11.

Third, the nation's capital offers unique resources for understanding post-September 11 civil rights and civil liberties issues of relevance to the entire country. While the forum was concerned first and foremost with the local situation, the Committee was aware that given trends across the United States, addressing local issues in isolation would not make sense; thus the decision was made to look also at the larger, national context of civil rights and civil liberties concerns after September 11. The metropolitan Washington, D.C., area is home to key federal agencies and to an array of national organizations, including civil rights, legal, and advocacy groups that are playing a role in the public debate on these issues. Panelists from these agencies and organizations put current issues in their historical context and related events in the local area to nationwide trends.

In identifying the populations most affected by post-September 11 civil rights concerns, the Committee decided to concentrate on four overlapping communities: Arabs, South Asians, Muslims, and Sikhs, groups that bore the brunt of hate violence and discrimination connected to the attacks. In addition, the Committee identified Muslim women as a population with special concerns; among other reasons, the distinctive headscarves worn by some made them particularly visible targets for the backlash.

The Committee formed in late fall 2001 consisted of the chairpersons of the District of Columbia, Maryland, and Virginia Advisory Committees and three additional members of each committee. During the planning stage, the Committee concluded that in order to understand and address the civil rights and civil liberties concerns of the affected communities, it was necessary to develop a better understanding of Islam and of Muslim communities in the United States. Additionally, it was believed that an un-

derstanding of post-September 11 civil liberties issues would be enhanced by a historical review of how the United States has addressed civil liberties during national crises in the past, as well as an overview of the civil liberties ramifications of the USA Patriot Act[10] and its implementation.

In light of these considerations, the Inter-SAC Committee organized five panels on the following topics:

1. *Understanding Islam in America in the aftermath of September 11, 2001.* Specialists on Islam and on interfaith relations discussed the tenets of Islam and the current state of the faith, touching on Islamic ideas of justice, peace, warfare, and democracy. They sought to increase the public's awareness of Muslim communities in the United States, addressing specific stereotypes, misunderstandings, and policy issues that have affected relations between Muslims and people of other faiths.

2. *National crises, civil rights protections, and civil liberties: A historical review.* Two specialists in the area of civil liberties and law enforcement reviewed the impact of past national crises on civil rights and civil liberties protections in order to provide historical perspective on the relationship between civil liberties and national security in the aftermath of September 11.

3. *Implementing the USA Patriot Act of 2001: Civil rights impact.* This panel, which included representatives of law firms and civil liberties groups as well as two federal officials, examined the civil rights implications of laws, policies, and practices enacted or proposed by federal and local government agencies in the wake of the terrorist attacks, especially the potential impact of the USA Patriot Act. Special attention was given to the questioning and detention of Arab and Muslim men by federal authorities; immigration practices and procedures; air travel security procedures; new missions and policies of federal agencies; and oversight of federal agency activities.

---

[10] Uniting and Strengthening America by Providing Appropriate Tools Required to Intercept and Obstruct Terrorism Act of 2001, Pub. L. No. 107-56, 115 Stat. 272 (2001) (hereinafter USA PATRIOT Act).

4. *Fears and concerns of affected, at-risk communities.* Panelists from organizations representing Muslim, Sikh, Arab, and South Asian communities in the United States, as well as Muslim women, discussed the experiences of these communities in the aftermath of September 11, focusing both on hate crimes and discrimination and on civil liberties concerns as a result of federal policies and actions.

5. *Local government responses and best practices.* The panel examined the efforts of state and local government agencies in the Washington, D.C., metropolitan area to stem the surge in bias incidents and protect the rights and well-being of affected communities in their jurisdictions. The panel included representatives of local government agencies in Maryland and Virginia, a community relations specialist from the U.S. Department of Justice, and staff members of two Islamic educational organizations. They gave special attention to examples of best practices by public and private bodies in counteracting hate violence, religious bigotry, ethnic and racial discrimination, and denial of civil rights after September 11.

Organization of This Report

This introduction will be followed by seven chapters:

- Chapter 2: Background information on the affected population groups, clarifying who is included under the various designations and briefly presenting selected demographic and socioeconomic information on these communities in the United States.

- Chapter 3: A summary of Panel One on understanding Islam in America.

- Chapter 4: A summary of Panel Two on national crises and civil liberties in historical perspective.

- Chapter 5: A summary of Panel Three on the civil rights impact of the USA Patriot Act.

- Chapter 6: A summary of Panel Four on the fears and concerns of affected communities.

- Chapter 7: A summary of Panel Five on local government responses and best practices.

- Chapter 8: A summary of key observations based on the forum testimony and limited additional research.

The timeframe covered by the report extends from September 11, 2001, through April 25, 2002. In a few cases, however, the report has been updated with relevant information that has become available since the forum.

In the reports from the panels, each panelist's presentation is briefly summarized, based on his or her initial statement as well as subsequent dialogue and answers to questions from Committee members and the audience. The summaries basically present each speaker's main points in the order they were made, although in some cases the order has been adjusted to facilitate topical organization. During the affected agency review process, presenters verified each summary for accuracy and some provided updates. In those cases where agencies were mentioned but not represented at the forum, the Inter-SAC Committee sought review of appropriate sections of the report from designated agency representatives.[11]

---

[11] In the case of the U.S. Department of Justice, the Inter-SAC Committee asked Paul Martin, of the department's Office of the Inspector General, who participated in the forum, to inform the Eastern Regional Office if there were additional offices at the department that should receive and review the report. No information of this nature was forwarded to the Eastern Regional Office.

Chapter 2

Background on Arab, South Asian, Muslim, and Sikh Communities in the United States

In planning the forum, the Inter-SAC Committee decided to focus on four overlapping communities in the national capital area that have been most severely affected by hate violence and discrimination related to September 11: Arabs, South Asians, Muslims, and Sikhs. These "communities" are understood in their broadest sense, as including not only noncitizen immigrants but also naturalized U.S. citizens and U.S.-born Americans of these backgrounds. In addition, the Committee identified Muslim women as a population with special concerns.

It is important at the outset to stress that the various labels, used at times indiscriminately in the media and in popular discourse, have distinct meanings and are not interchangeable. "Arab" refers to language and culture; "Muslim" and "Sikh" refer to religion; while "South Asian" (like "Middle Eastern"[1]) refers to region of origin. There is, of course, considerable overlap between the populations: for example, many—but not all—Arabs are also Muslims. Panelists noted that some Americans are confused about the various labels, believing, for example, that "Muslim" and "Arab" mean the same thing,[2] or that turban-wearing Sikhs are Arab and Muslim when in fact they are neither.

This chapter briefly profiles each of the four main groups, explaining who is included and presenting selected data on the size, geographic distribution, and characteristics of each of these communities in the Washington, D.C., metropolitan area and nationwide. It should be noted, however, that it is very difficult to gauge the size of these populations, either nationally or locally. U.S. census data can in some cases provide rough estimates, but the census tends to undercount minority groups, and in any case does not ask about religious affiliation.

Arabs

Arabs are people who speak Arabic as their first language, numbering more than 200 million worldwide.[3] The "Arab world" consists of 22 countries in the Middle East and North Africa where Arabic is the principal (although not the only) language spoken.[4] Arabs are united by language, culture, and history, but they are religiously diverse: most Arabs are Muslims, but there are also millions of Christian Arabs and thousands of Jewish Arabs.

---

[1] Although used frequently in policy contexts, the term "Middle Eastern" is too broad to be a useful population identifier for the purposes of this report. "The Middle East" is a loose designation referring to Southwest Asia along with parts of North Africa, and is usually taken to include the Arabic-speaking countries from Egypt east to the Persian Gulf, plus Israel and Iran and sometimes Turkey. People who live in this region are diverse in language, culture, and religion. *See* American-Arab Anti-Discrimination Committee, "Facts About Arabs and the Arab World," <http://www.adc.org/index.php?id=248> (July 23, 2002).

[2] Yahya Hendi, testimony before the District of Columbia, Maryland, and Virginia Advisory Committees to the U.S. Commission on Civil Rights, community forum, Annandale,

Virginia, April 24–25, 2002, transcript, p. 23 (hereafter cited as Forum Transcript).

[3] American-Arab Anti-Discrimination Committee, "Facts About Arabs and the Arab World."

[4] Algeria, Bahrain, the Comoros Islands, Djibouti, Egypt, Iraq, Jordan, Kuwait, Lebanon, Libya, Mauritania, Morocco, Oman, Palestine, Qatar, Saudi Arabia, Somalia, Sudan, Syria, Tunisia, the United Arab Emirates, and Yemen. Iran and Turkey are not Arab countries (their primary languages are Farsi and Turkish, respectively). Nor, of course, is Afghanistan, notwithstanding some confusion in the U.S. public on this point. American-Arab Anti-Discrimination Committee, "Facts About Arabs and the Arab World."

Arabic-speaking people have come to the United States in several major waves, beginning in the late 19th century. Although they share a common linguistic and cultural heritage, Arab Americans are a highly diverse group. While all Arab countries have sent emigrants to this country, the majority of Arab Americans today are of Lebanese, Syrian, Egyptian, or Palestinian descent.[5] About three-quarters of Arab Americans are Christians (Catholic, Orthodox, and Protestant),[6] many descended from the first major wave that consisted mainly of Syrian and Lebanese merchants.[7] Only about a quarter of the Arab American population is Muslim. However, a second wave of Arab immigration that started after World War II is predominantly Muslim, making Muslims the fastest-growing segment of the Arab American community.[8]

Although the 2000 census reported about 1.25 million Americans of Arab ancestry, other researchers put the total at around 3 million.[9] Eighty-two percent of persons of Arab descent in the United States are U.S. citizens, and 63 percent were born in this country;[10] contrary to the stereotypes, Arab Americans are by no means completely or even mainly an immigrant group.[11]

The Arab American population is overwhelmingly urban, and Washington, D.C., is one of the top five metropolitan areas where this population resides; the others are Los Angeles, Detroit, New York-New Jersey, and Chicago.[12] In the national capital area, the largest concentrations are in suburban Fairfax County, Virginia, and Montgomery County, Maryland.

As a group, Arab Americans are relatively young, have education and income above the U.S. average, and work mainly in white-collar occupations; many are small-business owners. Diverse in their party affiliations, Arab Americans have held public office at many levels.[13]

South Asians

South Asians originate in the countries of the South Asian subcontinent, that is, India, Pakistan, Bangladesh, Sri Lanka, Nepal, Bhutan, and Maldives. (Afghanistan is not properly considered part of South Asia, although there are close ties.) South Asians are linguistically, culturally, and religiously diverse, with large populations of Muslims, Hindus, and Sikhs, as well as many religious minorities.

The first significant South Asian immigration to the United States occurred around the turn of the 20th century, when Indian laborers, mainly Sikhs, made their way to California and the Pacific Northwest in response to recruitment by railroad, steamship, and lumber companies.[14] Congress barred immigration from Asia between 1918 and 1946, but immigration from across South Asia greatly accelerated with the immigration reform of 1965. Today there are at least 2 million people of South Asian ancestry in the United States. Indians are by far the largest group, with 1.7 million people reporting Indian origin in the 2000 census; Pakistanis are second largest.[15] Some other researchers and organizations believe the totals to be much higher than the census figures indicate.[16] In the Washington,

[5] Arab American Institute Foundation, "Arab American Population Highlights," <http://www.aaiusa.org/educational _packet.htm> (Oct. 27, 2002).

[6] Catholic includes Roman Catholic, Maronite, and Melkite (Greek Catholic) rites; Orthodox includes Antiochian, Syrian, Greek, and Coptic rites; and Muslim includes Sunni, Shi'a, and Druze. Zogby International Survey, February 2000, cited in Arab American Institute Foundation, "Arab American Population Highlights."

[7] Samia El-Badry, "The Arab-American Market," *American Demographics,* January 1994.

[8] Helen Hatab Samhan, "Who Are Arab Americans?" <http://www.aaiusa.org/educational_packet.htm> (Oct. 27, 2002).

[9] Arab American Institute, "Census Figures on Arab Population in U.S. Give Partial Glimpse at Community," press release, June 5, 2002.

[10] Arab American Institute Foundation, "Quick Facts About Arab Americans," <http://www.aaiusa.org/educational_packet. htm> (Oct. 27, 2002).

[11] Attorney Albert Mokaiber, a member of the forum audience, commented: "I'm a fourth-generation Arab American. My grandfather was in World War I, my father World War II, my brother during Vietnam, and I have two nephews on active duty now. We do not need to take a political litmus test. We're solid citizens." Forum Transcript, p. 403.

[12] Arab American Institute Foundation, "Quick Facts About Arab Americans."

[13] Samhan, "Who Are Arab Americans?"

[14] Indian American Center for Political Awareness, "Indian American History" and "Indian American Immigration," <http://iacfpa.org/census2k/iahist.htm> (Oct. 19, 2002).

[15] U.S. Census Bureau, "The Asian Population: 2000," February 2002, <www.census.gov/prod/2002pubs/c2kbr01-16. pdf> (Oct. 18, 2002).

[16] For example, Neeta Bhasin of ASB Communications, a New York-based agency specializing in the South Asian market, estimates there are 4 million South Asians in the

D.C., metropolitan area the Census Bureau estimates 152,655 South Asians, including 83,642 in Virginia, 65,769 in Maryland, and 3,244 in the District of Columbia.[17]

Among South Asians in this country, the large Indian American community stands out as particularly well educated and prosperous, with education and income levels that exceed those of U.S.-born whites.[18] Many are professionals, especially doctors, scientists, engineers, and financial analysts, and there are also a large number of entrepreneurs. The five urban areas with the largest Indian populations include the Washington/Baltimore metropolitan area as well as New York, Chicago, Los Angeles, and San Francisco.[19]

Muslims

Muslims are followers of Islam. One of the three major monotheistic religions in the world, Islam calls for complete acceptance of and submission to the teachings and guidance of God. Anyone may become a Muslim, regardless of gender, race, or nationality, by reciting a declaration of faith and embracing a lifestyle in accord with Islamic principles. Specific acts, including fasting, daily prayer, and the pilgrimage to Mecca, are considered the pillars of Muslim spiritual life.[20]

There are an estimated 1.2 billion Muslims worldwide. They live in every world region and belong to many different cultures and ethnic groups. The 10 countries with the largest Muslim populations, in descending order, are Indonesia, Pakistan, Bangladesh, India, Turkey, Iran, Egypt, Nigeria, and China.[21] Of these, only Egypt is an Arab country, and despite the stereotypes, only 193 million of the world's Muslims—15 to 18 percent of the total—are Arabs.[22]

Although the presence of Muslims in the United States dates back to the 1500s, the first major wave of Muslim immigration took place in the late 19th century, with arrivals from Syria, Lebanon, Jordan, and other Arab lands.[23] Immigration of Muslims from many countries accelerated after 1965 and continues apace, as do conversions of U.S.-born Americans to Islam. Estimates of the current number of Muslims in the United States vary from as low as 1.5 million to as high as 6–7 million, the latter figure being accepted by major Muslim organizations.[24] The number of mosques in this country has grown by 25 percent in the past seven years and now totals more than 1,200.[25]

The Muslim population in this country is ethnically diverse. Immigrant Muslims come mainly from the South Asian and Arab countries, with smaller numbers from Africa, Iran, Turkey, and Southeast Asia.[26] There is also a growing population of American-born converts to Islam, most of them African Americans, making up perhaps a third of the total population of Muslims in the United States.[27] The 10 states

---

country, including 2.2 million Indians and 1 million Pakistanis; these estimates are derived from research by various organizations. Personal communication, Sept. 12, 2002.

[17] Lobenstine testimony, Forum Transcript, p. 18.

[18] Based on data from the 2000 census, cited in Indian American Center for Political Awareness, "Income, Education, and Occupation," <http://iacfpa.org/census2k/iadem.htm> (Oct. 19, 2002).

[19] Based on data from the 2000 census, cited in Indian American Center for Political Awareness, "Indian American Population in the Largest Metropolitan Areas in the United States," <http://iacfpa.org/census2k/census2000metropop.htm> (Oct. 19, 2002).

[20] The two main branches of Islam, Sunni and Shi'a, have some doctrinal differences between them. Worldwide, 85–90 percent of Muslims are Sunnis. Each of these primary branches of Islam contains several different "schools" or sub-branches. In addition, Sufism is a form of Islamic mysticism which, although a small minority, has greatly influenced the faith. For more information about the doctrines and practices of Islam, see Council on Islamic Education, "About Islam and Muslims," <http://www.cie.org/About_Islam.html> (Oct. 17, 2002), and American-Arab Anti-Discrimination Committee, "Facts About Islam," <http://www.adc.org/index.php?id=249> (Sept. 9, 2002). See also the summary of Panel One.

[21] American-Arab Anti-Discrimination Committee, "Facts About Arabs and the Arab World."

[22] Council on Islamic Education, "About Islam and Muslims."

[23] Ibid.

[24] Bill Broadway, "Number of U.S. Muslims Depends on Who's Counting," Washington Post, Nov. 24, 2001; Gustav Niebuhr, "Studies Suggest Lower Count for Number of U.S. Muslims," New York Times, Oct. 25, 2001. Figures are uncertain, in part because the U.S. census does not ask about religious affiliation.

[25] Council on American-Islamic Relations, "The Mosque in America: A National Portrait," <http://www.cair-net.org/mosquereport/> (Oct. 27, 2002).

[26] A survey by the Council on American-Islamic Relations found that at the average mosque, 33 percent of members are of South Asian origin, 30 percent are African American, and 25 percent are from the Arabic-speaking world. See "The Mosque in America: A National Portrait."

[27] Abdul-Malik testimony, Forum Transcript, p. 311. Estimates of the percentage of U.S. Muslims who are African

with the largest Muslim populations, in order, are California, New York, Illinois, New Jersey, Indiana, Michigan, Virginia, Texas, Ohio, and Maryland.[28] In the Washington, D.C., metropolitan area, according to one researcher's estimates, there are 60,000 to 70,000 immigrant Muslims and 25,000 African American Muslims.[29]

A recent survey of Muslims across the United States found this population to be predominantly young, well educated, and concentrated in professional, managerial, and technical occupations.[30] Eight in 10 respondents were registered to vote,[31] and of those registered, 85 percent said they were very likely to vote. Large majorities expressed support for robust participation in American life, including involvement with civic, charitable, and professional organizations, while also reporting that they are active at their mosque or other religious organization.

Sikhs

Sikhs are followers of the Sikh religion. Founded in the Punjab region of India in the 15th century, Sikhism is a monotheistic faith that retains some elements of Islam and Hinduism while also defining important differences from them (rejecting, for example, the caste system). It is the fifth largest religion in the world with an estimated 23 million adherents,[32] the majority of them in India, although there has been a substantial diaspora to other areas of the world. Sikhs wear distinctive dress to signify commitment to their faith, including uncut hair covered by a turban and a small ceremonial sword known as a *kirpan*. All Sikh men include "Singh" in their surnames and all Sikh women include "Kaur."

Although often perceived as foreign because of their turbans, Sikhs have lived in the United States for more than a hundred years. Sikh immigrants first came to the Pacific Coast states around the turn of the 20th century to build railroads, farm, or work in mills and foundries.[33] Later, as Asian immigration picked up after 1965, Sikhs arrived in sizable numbers in various parts of the country. Although no firm figures are available, the number of Sikhs in the United States today is estimated at around 500,000, with some 6,000 to 8,000 in the Washington, D.C., metropolitan area.[34] Although Sikh Americans, like others from South Asia and the Middle East, endured discrimination in employment and education,[35] they have "not only prospered in business, industry, and the professions; they are also beginning to participate in the political life" of the country of their adoption.[36]

American vary. In addition to the survey cited above by the Council on American-Islamic Relations, which found 30 percent African Americans among mosque members, a recent survey of U.S. Muslims by Zogby International found 20 percent of the respondents identifying themselves as African American, but the survey sample was small. *See* Project MAPS: Muslims in American Public Square and Zogby International, "American Muslim Poll," November/December 2001, <www.projectmaps.com> (Oct. 27, 2002).

[28] Council on Islamic Education, "About Islam and Muslims."

[29] Estimates by Sulayman Nyang, principal investigator with Project MAPS: Muslims in American Public Square, cited in Lobenstine testimony, Forum Transcript, p. 16.

[30] Researchers interviewed 1,781 Muslim adults in November–December 2001. *See* Project MAPS, "American Muslim Poll."

[31] Of the 21 percent of respondents who were not registered, half said it was because they were not U.S. citizens, while the other half gave varying reasons.

[32] Singh testimony, Forum Transcript, p. 325.

[33] Library of the University of California at Berkeley, "Echoes of Freedom: South Asian Pioneers in California, 1899–1965," <http://www.lib.berkeley.edu/SSEAL/echoes/toc.html> (Oct. 27, 2002).

[34] Singh testimony, Forum Transcript, p. 325.

[35] Ranbir S. Sandhu, "Sikhs in America: Stress and Survival," in *Recent Researches in Sikhism*, eds., Jasbir S. Mann and Kharak S. Mann (Patiala, India: Punjab University, 1992). Available at <http://www.lib.ucdavis.edu/punjab/assim.html> (Oct. 27, 2002).

[36] Patwant Singh, *The Sikhs* (New York: Doubleday, 1999), p. 242. For example, in 1957 Dalip Singh Saund (D-CA) became the first Indian-American to be elected to the U.S. Congress, where he served for three terms.

Chapter 3

Understanding Islam in America in the Aftermath of September 11

The forum opened with a panel intended to increase understanding of the affected communities and Islam as a religion, addressing specific misunderstandings and stereotypes that have colored relations between Muslims and people of other faiths. Panelists included specialists on Islam as well as those focusing on interfaith relations. In their presentations, the panelists made the following key points, among others:

- Islam is a religion based on belief in one God and on concepts of peace, justice, and equity, and it has much in common with both Christianity and Judaism.

- Various stereotypes and misunderstandings about Muslims are prevalent, such as the notions that all Muslims are Arabs and vice versa, that Islam is fundamentally incompatible with democracy, and that Islam calls for the suppression of women.

- The history of the Christian crusades and European colonization of the Muslim world has led many Muslims worldwide to believe that the West wants to keep them oppressed.

- The overwhelming majority of Muslims in the United States condemned the terrorist acts and reject the notion that these acts are religiously justified by Islam or reflect the nature of the faith.

- While loyal to the United States, many Muslims in the United States disagree with aspects of U.S. policy in the Middle East, especially in relation to Iraq and the Israeli-Palestinian conflict.

- Recent government actions, particularly the detentions of Muslim men and the raids by federal agents on Muslim homes, have alienated and intimidated U.S. Muslims.

- There have been increased opportunities for dialogue between Muslims and Americans of other faiths since September 11 resulting in fruitful interfaith contacts such as joint prayer services, panel discussions, and public statements.

Yahya Hendi
Muslim chaplain, Georgetown University, and imam, Islamic Society of Frederick, Maryland

The word "Islam" means "peace" and also "surrender." Muslims believe that Islam teaches us to achieve peace in our lives by surrendering to the will of God and living up to the teachings of the prophets. We are created in God's image and are called to represent God on earth spiritually, morally, and physically. Islam, Judaism, and Christianity have much in common—belief in one God, the legacy of the prophets, many biblical events, and the concept of peace as an ultimate goal. We also share a historical space and time, and the social and political challenges of our time.

There are several prevalent misunderstandings about Islam. First of all, many people think that if you are Muslim you must be Arab, and if you are Arab you must be Muslim, but that's not true. Worldwide, there are more than 1 billion Muslims who are not Arabs. At the same time, there are many Arabs who are Christian or Jewish.

Second, many people seem to think, based on what the Taliban has done, that Islam by nature abuses women. I think that to the contrary, Islam gives to women the rights it gives to men.

Third, people fail to differentiate between political and religious agendas. Often religion is used to back up a political agenda, as bin Laden did, and as the Christian crusades did in history.

Fourth, people counterpose "Islam and the West," as if there were no Muslims in the West. With millions of Muslims living in North America and Europe, Muslims are part of the fabric of Western society. I see myself as an American Muslim; although I was born in another part of the world, the West is my home.

As spokesperson for the Islamic Jurisprudence Council of North America, I believe there's no contradiction between Islam and democracy. For something to become an order under Islamic law, it must ensure the safeguarding and protection of, one, the intellect and freedom of expression of every person who lives under Islamic law; two, every person's right to accumulate wealth; three, every person's dignity; and four, every person's freedom of religious expression. Islamic law says that people should be governed by an elected body, and that elected body decides on what is good or bad for the community, as long as it does not contradict the four points I just mentioned. The foundations of democracy are not in opposition to the foundations of Islamic teachings.

There is nothing in Islamic law that prevents a Muslim from turning away from Islam.[1] This question was addressed recently by the Islamic Jurisprudence Council of North America, which recognized that such conversions have happened in our history and that the individuals were left free to live under Islamic rule. Have there been violations of this? Certainly; but other faiths have also engaged in similar persecution at times. We should not accuse Islam of being responsible for intolerant actions because the individuals who carry out these actions happen to be Muslim; nor should intolerant actions by some Christians and Jews reflect on their religion.

The September 11 attacks have forced some soul-searching in the Muslim community. But in each religious community, not only in ours, the majority opinion has been silent while the extreme minority has been loud. We, the majority,

need to become more vocal. A Muslim article of faith is to enjoin the good and forbid the evil; during Ramadan, we go through self-criticism of our own actions.

What really frustrated the community was that the Muslims who were targeted by the federal raids in March were not the people known to have extreme agendas.[2] For instance, Dr. al Alwani,[3] who had traveled from mosque to mosque telling Muslims that America is the best country in the world, who had issued a *fatwa* urging Muslims to fight in the U.S. military in Afghanistan against terrorism, was targeted. His house was raided and his wife was forced to remain for seven hours in her sleeping clothes, not allowed to cover her head. Cupboards were broken, TVs were broken. Every Muslim in this country knows what happened to Dr. al Alwani. What kind of message is that sending?

On the positive side, I have recently seen a great deal of success in interfaith dialogue that I had not seen before September 11. After September 11, churches and synagogues were opened for Muslims to go in and celebrate their services. I have given more than 350 lectures at religious institutions since then, participating in dialogue with clergy of other faiths, trying to build mutual understanding. Leaders of three well-known Christian entities have asked their members to reach out to Muslims. If religious people are willing to follow the fundaments of their faiths, they will find more room for dialogue and interreligious relations because the fundaments of Judaism, Christianity, and Islam are the same.[4]

---

[1] Concerns have been reported to the U.S. Commission on Civil Rights about pressures being brought on individuals who convert from Islam to a non-Muslim faith. Imam Hendi's comments were made in response to a question about how such conversions are handled.

[2] On March 21–21, 2002, agents from a U.S. Treasury Department financial crimes task force, called "Operation Green Quest," served federal search warrants on 19 locations in Northern Virginia ("In Anti-Terrorist Raids, Issues of Tact and Tactics," *Washington Post*, Apr. 11, 2002, p. B05). In one of these raids on March 20, 2002, one Pakistani woman, who came to the United States in 1970 and long ago became a naturalized citizen, and her 18-year-old daughter were confronted by armed men dressed in black who broke down their house door. When the daughter tried to call 911, "the men ordered the teenager at gunpoint to put down the phone, then kept both of them handcuffed for nearly five hours" ("VA Program Helping Muslim Women Upset by Post 9/11 Raids," *Washington Post*, Oct. 2, 2002, p. B04).

[3] Dr. Taha Jabir al Alwani, a noted scholar of Islamic jurisprudence, is president of the Graduate School of Islamic and Social Sciences in Leesburg, Virginia.

[4] Yahya Hendi, summary of testimony before the District of Columbia, Maryland, and Virginia Advisory Committees to the U.S. Commission on Civil Rights, community forum,

Sanaulla Kirmani

Adjunct professor of philosophy and religion,
Goucher College

Christianity is based on the idea of love; that does not necessarily mean that all Christians love everybody else all the time, but there is a fundamental picture of God as love in Christianity. The fundamental idea in Islam is of a God of justice; that does not necessarily mean that every Muslim is just, but that the primary idea in most Muslim social and economic affairs is that of promoting justice. God implies unity because Muslims are vehemently monotheistic, and that implies also for Muslims the idea of peace, because everything in this world surrenders to God and is at peace with God. That does not necessarily mean that every individual Muslim is a person of peace, but that Muslims as a culture have the idea of peace in their minds.

Muslims are keenly aware of equity in human relations, including the distribution of wealth. The Quran says that men and women are created from the same source and have no difference in their intellectual capacities; they may have different stations in life.[5]

September 11 has sometimes been depicted as something that is justified by Muslims and Islam, as if all Muslims were somehow responsible for this horrible event. But looking at it in historical perspective, we may recall that with the expansion of Islam the rules of warfare changed to prohibit scorched earth and killing of unarmed civilians. Islam radically changed the idea and practice of warfare, so that no killing of common people ever took place under Islamic rules and regulations. Therefore it strikes Muslims as very, very bizarre to hear that the September 11 attacks are somehow representative of Islam. American Muslims have tried to show people here, those who will listen, that these at-

---

Annandale, Virginia, April 24–25, 2002, transcript, pp. 19–26, 64, 82–83, 85–86, 102–03, 109, 115–16, 124–26 (hereafter cited as Forum Transcript).

[5] Referring to Mr. Kirmani's statement, a SAC member later questioned whether having different stations in life for men and women was compatible with democracy. In response, panelist Clark Lobenstine of the InterFaith Conference noted that many fundamentalist Christians believe strongly in men and women having different stations in life, yet their commitment to democracy is not questioned. Similar perspectives on male and female roles, he noted, are found in some areas of Judaism, Christianity, Islam, and other faiths. Forum Transcript, pp. 111–12.

tacks were not religious events, but expressions of some kind of frustration.

To raise the question of whether there is a radical difference between Islam and the West reflects the erroneous notion that Muslims are fundamentally different from people of other faiths. There is a radical difference between those of us sitting here at this table: some of us were raised in Michigan, others in the South, others in Massachusetts, and we do have some cultural differences. Muslims also have these kinds of differences among themselves. But it is not necessarily the case that a Muslim is altogether different from a Christian, Jew, Hindu, or Sikh.

Islam has no central ecclesiastical authority to tell people what is right and wrong, or to make corrections if things go in a wrong direction. There can be and are differences of opinion. That's why Islam is suited to democracy—but sometimes democracy is not allowed to grow in Islamic countries. Colonialism and anticommunism have had unfortunate impacts on the historical development of Islam. The impact of colonization throughout the Muslim world meant that almost any idea associated with colonialism or the colonizers was rejected. Furthermore, for expedient purposes of fighting communism, people who were otherwise rational supported governments that were dictatorial. That is a tragedy, I think, in Islamic and Muslim countries. And our name as Americans, as the United States, has become associated with some of those dictatorial governments.

Recent events and the government's response have sent a chill through the Muslim community. Children are afraid to admit they are Muslims in school. Adults are reluctant to get involved in community activities, or even to talk on the phone, thinking it's tapped. Some are afraid to attend Friday prayers.

It is essential to promote dialogue between Muslims and non-Muslims, and our country, the United States, perhaps more than other countries, provides an environment where this can happen. For example, I recently attended a "peace seder" at a university in Towson, Maryland, where Jews and Muslims celebrated a seder together. I think most of the difficulties we have are because we think of each other as strangers. We especially need to reach out to those who are most intolerant.[6]

Yvonne Haddad

Center for Muslim-Christian Understanding, Georgetown University

After the attacks, Americans asked, "Why do they hate us?" Immediately we had a parade of people come on TV and tell us why they hated us. They hated us because of our values, we were told; they hated us because of our democracy, because of our very existence. Every one of those people who told us what to believe was a policymaker, and every one of them said it isn't because of our policies.

But if you look at Mohammed Atta's will and at bin Laden's statements, you will see that they identified three policies that are repugnant to them. One is our policy on Iraq. In the Arab world, they still remember when former Secretary of State Albright was asked about the 500,000 Iraqi children who die every year because of our policy of containment. She said, "Yes, it's tough, but it's worth it." Those three words, "it's worth it," still reverberate throughout the Muslim world. Five hundred thousand children can die and we don't care.

A second policy they identified is our policy in Palestine, which has become an issue for Muslims worldwide. And the third policy is the presence of U.S. troops in Saudi Arabia.

I am not justifying what happened on September 11. Many Muslims throughout the world are not justifying what happened, but they are saying we need to look at U.S. policies in the Middle East. Their question is, "Why does America hate Islam?"

There are 1,400 years of relationship between Muslims and Christians or the West. They include the Crusades, which were based on the idea that if you killed an infidel—in this case, the infidel is the Muslim—you go straight to heaven; you get an expiation. The history includes the Inquisition in Spain, when Muslims were told to convert, leave, or die. It includes colonialism, when European powers, starting in the 16th century, expanded all over the Muslim world. Today, of the 56 Muslim countries in the world, only two have not been occupied by European countries.

Muslims are aware of this historical relationship and many believe that the West wants their resources, wants to keep them oppressed. President Bush's recent comment about mounting a "crusade," and Secretary Powell's comments about "we, the civilized world," reinforced that notion. We don't know if the President's remark about a crusade was a slip of the tongue or a Freudian slip. But Muslims heard: "Here they come again. They hate us; they want to destroy us."

Arabs immigrating to the United States initially were not allowed to become citizens. Eventually they were accepted, and Arab Americans fought with the American forces in World War I, World War II, Korea, Vietnam, and the Gulf War. Dearborn, Michigan, has a center for Veterans of Foreign Wars whose members are all Arab Muslims. The influx of new immigrants after 1965 has brought in many Arab professionals who are helping our economy—doctors and computer scientists and others. Do they feel at home in America? They did. But after September 11 it has become very, very difficult.

Arab Americans have no access to policymaking and feel disenfranchised. Money they donate to candidates is returned because of the stigma. It's not just a question of assimilation.

With the USA Patriot Act, Arab Americans and Muslims are being specifically targeted as threatening elements in society. The March raids in Northern Virginia targeted people the U.S. government recognized as Muslim leaders; then included the school that produced the Muslim chaplains for the U.S. military. It also targeted Dr. al Alwani, who issued a *fatwa* to Muslims to go fight in the war against terrorism. His home was ransacked by federal agencies in March.

President Bush asked Americans not to stereotype Muslims and Arab Americans, but there's a difference between his words and the actions of the Justice Department. The Muslim community worldwide fears that the U.S. has declared war on Islam. They don't see it as a war on terrorism.

In the 20th century, Islam became a modern religion: it deemphasized predestination, Muslims took on the burden of history and responsibility to act for change. They created resistance movements against European colonization. Bin

---

[6] Summary of testimony by Sanaulla Kirmani, Forum Transcript, pp. 26–32, 62–64, 76–79, 80–81, 88–89, 123–24.

Laden represents a type of Islam that was developed to fight communism, encouraged by the U.S. government. The United States supported, trained, and armed bin Laden's movement as a wall against the spread of communism.

We hang on to stereotypes about how Islam treats women. You can't generalize from the practices in one country, such as Saudi Arabia or Afghanistan.[7]

Nedzib Sacirbey
Interim director, American Muslim Council

Islam values peace; the traditional greeting, *as-salaam alaikum,* means "peace upon you." Muslims support peace for all; we believe that all humans are equal in creation. There is no difference between Muslim and non-Muslim. We have one creator, and life is the gift of our creator. We believe in accountability for our actions: we will, on the day of judgment, answer to our creator for everything we do. Islam condemns suicide and homicide because life belongs to human beings as a gift of God.

I'm European, from Bosnia-Herzegovina; I'm not Arab or Middle Eastern. There are about 200,000 Bosnian Muslims in this country. I came to the United States because I wanted freedom; I was jailed during the German occupation and again during the communist regime. I chose a country of freedom and I came with faith in America.

In 1941 President Roosevelt spoke about four freedoms, including freedom of speech and expression, freedom of faith and worship, and freedom from fear. I'm determined to try to see what is best in America as well as to remind myself what has sometimes been wrong in America in the past. Slavery was wrong; lynching was wrong. Discrimination is wrong, and probably some elements of this so-called USA Patriot Act are wrong today. And we have to be open to say so.

American Muslims are part of America; without us, America will be smaller. We have adopted America and we love America. We consider ourselves American patriots. One reason is that most Muslims here come from countries of Asia and Africa that were colonies—but not American colonies—and they respect America because it never was a colonial power.

But this question about Iraq. Muslims hate Saddam Hussein and would like him to disappear from the political scene, but without paying 10,000 Iraqi lives. Second, Palestine.

There is no Muslim organization in this country that did not condemn the al Qaeda terrorist attack, and many have given contributions to the fight against al Qaeda. Al Qaeda is an ulcer on the body of Muslims, and we want it to disappear as soon as possible because it gives a face to Muslims that is not our face. But we do have a problem with this question about Palestine. We support the Oslo agreement, and America supported it, but Sharon was always against it. President Bush says Sharon is a man of peace. I don't know how many Americans think so but I know the rest of the world thinks Sharon is a man of war, an enemy of peace and he is accused of war crimes.

Muslims in the United States didn't come here to impose Islamic law, but to obey American law and the Constitution. We want to add to the diversity of America and practice our faith on the basis of American law.

In Dayton, I visited a beautiful mosque and a Muslim school, by name, Bright Horizons School. I found there a handwritten certificate of friendship, stating: "The members of Peace Lutheran Church want to assure the staff and members of the mosque that we are grateful that they are part of the Beaver Creak community and that we will not tolerate any unloving words, actions, or attitudes from anyone seeking to harm or intimidate them. Scripture tells us to love our neighbors as we love ourselves and to work hard at living in peace with everyone. We want students of Bright Horizons School to know they are loved. And we pray that we will all be able to live in peace with each other."

This is America.[8]

Clark Lobenstine
Executive director, InterFaith Conference of Metropolitan Washington

The InterFaith Conference of Metropolitan Washington began working in 1978 to bring Muslim, Protestant, Catholic, and Jewish communities together to increase understanding and

---

[7] Summary of testimony by Yvonne Haddad, Forum Transcript, pp. 32–41, 58–61, 71–76, 99–100, 113–14.

[8] Summary of testimony by Nedzib Sacirbey, Forum Transcript, pp. 41–47, 66–68, 93–96, 122–23.

dialogue. Other faith communities have since joined as well.

The Conference issued a statement on September 11, expressing outrage and grief over the terrorist attacks and stating that religion should not be used to justify violence, while also cautioning Americans not to rush to judgment as to the perpetrators. We held an interfaith prayer service on September 13 that was attended by more than 500 people.

Confronted with the rising tide of hate violence after September 11, we publicized the united stand of the religious community against expressions of religious bigotry. We worked with 18 key leaders from eight world religions, who joined in making an important statement and who stood with Muslim and Sikh victims of hate violence at the Islamic Center in Washington, D.C. That statement quoted the words of the Very Reverend Nathan Baxter, dean of the Washington National Cathedral: "Evil does not wear a turban, a tunic, a yarmulke, or a cross. Evil wears the garment of a human heart, a garment woven from the threads of hate and fear."

September 11 has presented an opportunity for public education about other faiths, especially Islam, and since that date there has been a surge in demand for speakers who can address this. Just since the beginning of 2002, we have worked with 30 congregations, schools, and community groups providing speakers and consulting on how to build bridges among faith traditions that are sometimes fighting elsewhere. The mainline Protestant congregations have been most active in hosting speakers of other faiths, so part of our challenge is to broaden that base and encourage more learning about other faiths within Islamic institutions, Catholic churches, and synagogues.

It has been said that "the world is most deeply divided not between those of different religions but between those of each religious tradition who hold their faith in an open-handed and generous way and those in each religious tradition who hold their faith in a closed-fisted and narrow way. It is the difference between those who feel firmly grounded in their faith by virtue of building walls and those who feel firmly grounded in their faith by virtue of deep roots."[9]

---

[9] Summary of testimony by Clark Lobenstine, Forum Transcript, pp. 47–57, 89–91, 105–07, 111–12.

Chapter 4

National Crises, Civil Rights, and Civil Liberties: A Historical Review

Panel Two heard from two specialists in the area of civil liberties and law enforcement, who discussed the impact of past national crises on civil rights and civil liberties protections in order to provide historical perspective on the situation in relation to September 11. They emphasized the following points:

- The current detentions and deportations of immigrants under antiterrorism statutes recall earlier events in U.S. history.

- Tactics currently being used—guilt by association, racial and religious profiling, secrecy, and exemption of government actions from oversight and accountability—were also used in past investigations, and have proven ineffective in identifying or preventing actual criminal activity.

- It is possible to have a successful antiterrorism strategy that fully respects the Constitution. Tactics that respect civil rights are more effective in getting at the truth.

Kit Gage
Director, First Amendment Foundation and National Committee Against Repressive Legislation

The history of how our government pursues what it understands as "politically based crime" varies little except in terms of who gets rounded up each time. In the Palmer raids, the government responded to the bombings that had taken place by rounding up thousands of immigrants and anarchists, holding them in jail, and deporting many of them, without ever bringing criminal proceedings against them.[1] They never found, and perhaps never really sought, the real perpetrators of the crimes. That was the not-so-honorable beginning of the FBI that J. Edgar Hoover was in charge of.

During World War II it was largely Japanese Americans who were rounded up and placed in detention without suspicion of having committed a crime. During the McCarthy era we saw the criminalizing of membership in organizations, apart from any criminal activity. The government has continued to find peaceful protest and political change movements dangerous even though the Constitution and Bill of Rights explicitly provide for them. In the 1960s, the Black Panther Party was destroyed by FBI activity through COINTELPRO.[2] Fred Hampton was murdered as a result of a collaboration between the FBI and the Chicago police department.[3] It's a very sad history in this country, but it's one that we have to understand clearly because it's a continuing, straight-line history.

Following COINTELPRO there was a movement to curb FBI abuses and protect First Amendment activity, resulting in part with the Pike and Church committee hearings in Congress and their comprehensive reports. However,

---

[1] The raids were conducted in 1919 by then Attorney General A. Mitchell Palmer in response to a rash of mail bombings.

[2] COINTELPRO, an acronym for "counterintelligence program," was a sweeping FBI domestic investigation that targeted a wide array of groups in the civil rights, antiwar, environmental, and women's movements between 1956 and 1971.

[3] Fred Hampton Sr., chairman of the Black Panther Party's Illinois chapter, was assassinated when police raided the Hampton's family apartment when all were asleep on December 4, 1969. The FBI had planted an informant in the group and worked with the Chicago police to plan the raid as part of COINTELPRO.

law enforcement still has difficulty understanding the difference between going after crime and going after association.

The 1996 antiterrorism act makes it a crime to give material support to organizations that the U.S. government, using very broad criteria, deems to be foreign terrorist organizations.[4] You can give diapers to an orphanage in an area that's under the control of a listed "foreign terrorist organization" and your gift of diapers is a crime under the 1996 law. The USA Patriot Act expands the penalties for that kind of activity.[5] Since 1996, the government has been using secret evidence to deny bond for people it wants to deport—detaining them for several years without charge and then trying to deport them. The secret evidence, when released, usually turns out to be garbage easily rebutted.

The USA Patriot Act massively increases government secrecy and further criminalizes dissent. People cannot learn the charges against them, and the government is keeping the courts out of appeals processes as lest people bring up the Bill of Rights or bar the use of secret evidence. The act also expands the government's authority to conduct covert searches, so-called sneak and peek, when federal agents search your home without your knowledge. Instead of going after the people who committed the terrorist crimes, the government largely seems to be going after people based on their ethnicity and religion. Arab Americans are being rounded up for questioning and deportation with no charges or allegations of criminal activity. This is not only discriminatory but is also poor law enforcement practice because it takes in too many people. We need to do something that is focused and works, not just round up the usual suspects.

The United States will never be able to stop all terrorist acts, just as we can't eliminate all crime by passing laws against it. We can try to minimize and prevent terrorism by going after the people whom we have information that they are planning or have committed such acts. If you allow due process—allow evidence to be seen and rebutted—you're more likely to get the right people. An organization should not be targeted just because it holds a position at odds with U.S.

foreign policy; the question should be, are the individuals engaging in criminal activity?

Cases are now being brought under habeas corpus for people detained. It took a while to figure out that people were being moved from all over the country to New Jersey to be deported right after September 11.[6] It was as though they had disappeared, and the government said it could not give out any information in order to protect their own "privacy." The families didn't know where they had gone.[7]

James X. Dempsey
Deputy director, Center for Democracy and Technology

Those of us who talk about civil liberties recognize the severity of the threat of terrorism. But we reject the idea that civil liberties and civil rights are at odds with national security, or that we can purchase security by giving up some of our civil liberties. History proves this to be incorrect. We need to find responses to terrorism that serve both civil liberties and national security interests.

Three tactics have been used time and again in history: (a) guilt by association, stereotyping, and targeting people by race, ethnicity, political beliefs, and religion; (b) secrecy; and (c) shielding of government action from oversight and accountability. These tactics were used with the detention of Japanese Americans during World War II, when the government said it had secret evidence of sabotage by Japanese Americans; years later, the government admitted there was no such evidence. They were used again in COINTELPRO, the counterintelligence program of the 1960s, and in the CISPES investigation in

---

[4] Antiterrorism and Effective Death Penalty Act of 1996, Pub. L. No. 104-132, 110 Stat. 1214 (1996).

[5] USA PATRIOT Act, Pub. L. No. 107-56 § 805, 115 Stat. 272 at 377 (2001).

[6] In November 2001 the Justice Department announced that 1,147 people had been detained on suspicion of terrorism, but refused to divulge the names of the individuals or the grounds for their arrests. In March 2002 the government began deporting the detainees, and by July 2002 it said all but 74 had been expelled to their home countries or, in a few cases, released to resume their lives in the United States. Susan Sachs, "U.S. Deports Most of Those Arrested in Sweeps After 9/11," *New York Times*, July 11, 2002.

[7] Kit Gage, summary of testimony before the District of Columbia, Maryland, and Virginia Advisory Committees to the U.S. Commission on Civil Rights, community forum, Annandale, Virginia, April 24–25, 2002, transcript, pp. 127–38, 154–55, 161–62, 165, 167, 170–72, 177–78 (hereafter cited as Forum Transcript).

the 1980s.[8] The CISPES probe became a nation-wide investigation of hundreds of groups and thousands of individuals, all conducted under the cloak of secrecy. Neither COINTELPRO nor the CISPES investigation turned up a single instance of anyone planning violence.

The 1996 antiterrorism act, passed in the wake of the Oklahoma City bombing and the first World Trade Center bombing, was also based on guilt by association, secret evidence, and exemption from oversight. The FBI and the Justice Department asserted strenuously to Congress that they knew who the terrorists were and could deport them, but couldn't let the evidence be shown in public, so they needed this secret proceeding. They got that authority, and used it to bring proceedings against 20 or 30 aliens. They told people, "We won't even tell you the name of the terrorist group you're alleged to be a member of because it's secret." How can you defend yourself against an allegation that you're a member of a group if the government won't even tell you what the group is? Lawyers challenged those cases in court and every one of them fell apart; judges looked at the evidence and said it doesn't add up. It was purely guilt by association.

But what was really outrageous about this was that while the government was engaged in its secret proceedings, 19 other people were in this country planning to hijack airplanes and fly them into the World Trade Center and the Pentagon, and they got away with it. They weren't religiously or politically active, so these secret, guilt-by-association, exempt-from-oversight procedures never found them. The critical point is that throughout our history, these tactics do not work. That has been proven time and again.

As a society, we've learned that government should have the law enforcement power it needs, but that there must be rules and constraints to ensure that that power is properly used. During the 1960s and 1970s, the courts became more active in enforcing the Bill of Rights. We passed the Freedom of Information Act (FOIA), limited intelligence agency operations in the United States, and imposed judicial oversight for wiretapping and other intrusive techniques. We created the concept of congressional oversight, and created nongovernmental watchdog organizations.

But since September 11, 2001, many of these constitutional checks and balances have been eliminated, pushed aside, or suspended. People have been in jail for six months on secret evidence, probably based on guilt by association. There has been a series of interviews based solely on ethnicity, age, and gender. There is a crackdown on access to information and an effort to avoid judicial and congressional oversight.[9]

This raises broader issues about the Freedom of Information Act and about the independence of the judiciary. Over the years, despite Congress' clear intent to cover national security information under the FOIA, the courts have almost always deferred to executive branch claims of national security as a basis for withholding information. So this reform, which has been extremely positive in many ways, has not been effectively enforced by the courts. Just as we saw judges become handmaidens to the war on drugs, I think that judges are not exercising the judicial role adequately in this instance. Over the years, judges who have suppressed evidence in drug cases or criticized government search-and-seizure activities have come under political criticism, and the message has gone out to the judiciary not to play that independent role. And so I think there needs to be constant defense of the power of an independent judiciary to stop executive branch actions that go too far.

Civil rights and civil liberties are not antithetical to an effective terrorism strategy, but are part of that strategy because tactics that respect civil rights are more effective in getting at the truth. We don't have judicial review just for the sake of filing lawsuits. Judicial review provides necessary scrutiny to prevent executive branch officials, who are acting under great pressure, from making decisions not based on sound evidence.

People should be held responsible for their individual actions. Rather than use guilt by association or ethnicity or religion, we need to do the hard work of identifying individuals engaged

---

[8] The CISPES investigation focused on the Committee in Solidarity with the People of El Salvador (CISPES), which opposed U.S. intervention in Central America.

[9] In December 2001 a coalition of civil liberties organizations filed a lawsuit under the Freedom of Information Act against the Department of Justice, seeking information about the hundreds of detainees being held in the antiterrorism investigation. Some information was released, but the government continued to withhold most of the information.

in criminal activity. How do we know we have the right people? We prove it in court, subject to cross-examination.

It is possible to have a successful antiterrorism strategy that fully respects the Constitution. Four key elements of such a strategy are (a) focus on criminal activity (including planning and conspiring) rather than on political or religious activity; (b) narrow the focus of the investigation rather than widen it; (c) ensure judicial review and control that covers the initiation of investigations, the use of investigative techniques, the holding of people, and the imposition of punishment; and (d) ensure oversight and accountability by Congress, internal review within the Justice Department, and a watchdog function by outside organizations.

Those who support civil rights and civil liberties should use what power and authority they have to ask questions—of government officials, of police who are cooperating with the FBI, of the Justice Department. How are they carrying out these activities, how many people are being held, and what for? Publish the answers you receive, and push your elected representatives to pursue these questions. Those who care about civil liberties must ask the effectiveness question: Are these policies really working?[10]

---

[10] Summary of testimony by James Dempsey, Forum Transcript, pp. 138–53, 156–64, 167, 171, 178–80.

Chapter 5

Implementing the USA Patriot Act of 2001: Civil Rights Impact

Panel Three looked in more detail at the implications of specific government policies and practices instituted after September 11, 2001. Several developments in the fall and winter of 2001 and the spring of 2002 alarmed civil rights advocates.[1] Within days of the attacks, the federal government began to pick up and detain men of Middle Eastern and South Asian descent in a nationwide dragnet, and by November 5, 2001, the U.S. Department of Justice (DOJ) announced that 1,147 people had been detained. The Justice Department refused to provide the most basic information, even to detainees' families, about who had been arrested, on what basis, and where they were being held. The detainees included U.S. citizens and legal residents as well as visa holders.[2] In December 2001, a coalition of civil liberties organizations filed a lawsuit seeking the release of information about the detainees.

Sweeping antiterrorism legislation known as the USA Patriot Act was rushed through Congress and signed into law on October 26, 2001. It gave the government broad new powers to detain noncitizens indefinitely and to conduct searches, seizures, and surveillance with reduced standards of cause and levels of judicial review, among other provisions. In addition, on October 31, 2001, the Justice Department published a new regulation allowing the government to eavesdrop on communications between attorneys and their clients without a court order.

Meanwhile, the Justice Department was also using the regulatory process to effect radical changes in the nation's immigration policies and enforcement practices, leading to the use of immigration law as a basis for picking up thousands of individuals and holding them in custody.

On November 9, 2001, Attorney General John Ashcroft announced a plan to interview 5,000 foreign men, ages 18 to 33, who had entered the United States from specified countries after January 1, 2000. The Justice Department directed state and local law enforcement to conduct the interviews, in which the men were questioned about their activities, studies, and travel, and asked to provide telephone numbers of their friends and relatives. While calling on the men to come forward for the "voluntary" interviews, the government also said that those questioned might be held without bond if investigators developed an interest in them or deported if they had violated immigration laws.

On November 13, 2001, President Bush issued a military order allowing the government to try noncitizens accused of terrorism-related charges in military tribunals, which lack many constitutional protections, rather than civilian courts.

On March 20–21, 2002, teams of federal agents headed by the U.S. Customs Service swept through Muslim homes, businesses, schools, and organizations in Northern Virginia in a series of raids known as Operation Green Quest. The raids frightened and angered the Muslim community as agents broke down doors, handcuffed people, and seized personal property ranging from computers to children's toys. The government maintained that it was searching for evidence of financial flows to terrorists abroad, but

---

[1] A more detailed summary, "ACLU Backgrounder: Chronology of the Assault on Civil Liberties Since September 11," is available from the American Civil Liberties Union.

[2] Statement of Kate Martin, director, Center for National Security Studies, before the Judiciary Committee of the United States Senate, 107th Cong., 1st session, on "DOJ Oversight: Preserving Our Freedoms While Defending Against Terrorism," Nov. 28, 2001, <http://judiciary.senate.gov/te11280lf-martin.htm> (Jan. 4, 2002).

Muslim groups vehemently denied such links and protested the tactics used by the agents in conducting the raids.[3]

Speakers on Panel Three included representatives of law firms and civil liberties groups, who discussed the problems faced by affected individuals, including their clients. Other speakers included representatives of the U.S. Department of Transportation and the U.S. Department of Justice.[4] Among the major points made by the speakers:

- The USA Patriot Act gives the government sweeping new enforcement powers, many of which had been sought by federal law enforcement long before September 11, but were rejected by Congress, and which are now being applied without meaningful judicial review. These new powers apply to all federal investigations, whether related to terrorism or not, and thus have very broad implications.

- Changes in immigration policies and procedures are potentially as important as the provisions of the USA Patriot Act. Many of the Arab and Muslim men who have been detained have been held on extremely technical visa violations that would not have been prosecuted before September 11.

- Many of the detainees have since been deported amid complete secrecy, effectively denying the individual's right to legal counsel.

- People of Arab and Muslim background are being treated as guilty unless they can prove themselves innocent.

- Ethnic, national, and religious discrimination is widespread within the nation's air travel system, even though the airlines have been advised by the Department of Transportation that such discrimination is illegal.

- Mechanisms are in place for members of the public to file complaints about discrimination in air travel, and these complaints are thoroughly investigated by federal agencies.

Laura W. Murphy

Director, Washington office, American Civil Liberties Union

The USA Patriot Act gives extensive new enforcement powers to the federal government. Most of its provisions apply to all federal investigations, not just those related to terrorism. In fact, September 11 gave the government an excuse to ram through a series of proposals that federal law enforcement had unsuccessfully sought for years to bolster routine drug cases and other nonterrorism investigations. Many provisions that Congress rejected when it considered antiterrorism legislation in 1996 subsequently reappeared in the USA Patriot Act.

Under the USA Patriot Act, sensitive information about U.S. citizens obtained through grand jury investigations and wiretaps can be disclosed to intelligence agencies without judicial review.[5] "Sneak and peak" warrants allow government agencies to conduct searches without telling the subject, so you can't assert your due process and Fourth Amendment rights.[6] The law makes it easier to compel private parties to release documents, including student records and personal financial records, and the government has broader powers to monitor Internet usage. There really isn't meaningful judicial review on many provisions of this law.

---

[3] Tom Jackman, "Raids Held in Terror Probe," *Washington Post*, Mar. 21, 2002; Tom Jackman and Brooke A. Masters, "More Sites Raided in Probe of Terrorism," *Washington Post*, Mar. 22, 2002; "In Anti-Terrorist Raids, Issues of Tact and Tactics," *Washington Post*, Apr. 11, 2002; Brooke A. Masters, "Va. Muslim Groups Want Property Back," *Washington Post*, May 3, 2002.

[4] Invitations were issued to several offices within the Justice Department in order to have panelists who could address the department's antiterrorism policies as well as those who could explain the department's efforts to respond to civil rights and civil liberties concerns. Among those invited, the Civil Rights Division, the Office of the Inspector General, and the Community Relations Service all sent representatives. However, the Office of Intergovernmental and Public Liaison, which communicates DOJ policies to the public, declined to participate.

Panelists from the Civil Rights Division, the Office of the Inspector General, and the Community Relations Service did not address the question of whether the antiterrorism policies and procedures being carried out by the department are necessary and effective. These panelists said this question could only be answered by staff of the Office of Intergovernmental and Public Liaison office.

[5] USA PATRIOT Act, Pub. L. No. 107-56 § 203, 115 Stat. 272 at 279 (2001).

[6] USA PATRIOT Act, Pub. L. No. 107-56 § 213, 115 Stat. 272 at 286 (2001).

The immigration provisions of the act are also very expansive. The attorney general can detain a noncitizen merely because he believes the person may be a threat to national security. A group of us who lobbied on the bill were able to get a reduction in the amount of time the attorney general can detain a noncitizen, but the administration has essentially ignored these restrictions in carrying out detentions since September 11.

The administration has also done other things of concern since the USA Patriot Act was enacted. It has issued regulations allowing government agencies to eavesdrop on attorney-client conversations without going to court to get a warrant. This applies to anyone in federal custody, not only those related to the September 11 investigation.

The government has also issued a military order calling for military tribunals for those detained in connection with September 11. Moreover, they are asserting the right to detain noncitizens at Guantánamo indefinitely even without bringing them before a tribunal, and to continue to detain people who have been acquitted by a tribunal.[7] So the government is flouting some provisions of the USA Patriot Act in its treatment of the detainees at Guantánamo. We have to fight hard to make habeas corpus available to people in custody under the USA Patriot Act; there is a strong feeling in Congress that habeas affords detainees the opportunity to bring frivolous claims, and we very much disagree with that.

In the current environment, the courts are unlikely to strike down the USA Patriot Act. So we have to look at cases where the law is applied in a way that violates constitutional rights, but this is difficult because much of the information the government is using is considered classified. Judges are reluctant to go up against the government when the government says it has classified information that provides a reason to detain an individual. So, we are engaged in painstaking litigation around detention policies under the Freedom of Information Act, but the attorney general has said he will deny FOIA requests that pertain to September 11. The constant alle-

gations that future terrorist acts are being planned make it very difficult to get any provisions of the Patriot legislation repealed; it will require a long-term effort to bring pressure on Congress. We want the United States to be safe but also to maintain its liberties.

Before September 11 we were making tremendous headway toward repealing the secret evidence provisions of the 1996 antiterrorism law, but this progress came to a halt after the attacks. Also, Congress was poised to pass antiracial profiling legislation, a bill that was developed with the input of civil liberties organizations, but that effort was also derailed and profiling is now being done much more. People are singled out, especially at airports and borders, because they are immigrants, have foreign-sounding names, are dark skinned, look foreign, or look like Muslims. This includes Sikhs because police can't tell the difference.[8]

Malea Kiblan

Immigration attorney, Kiblan & Battles

I have been retained by the Embassy of Saudi Arabia to secure legal assistance for their nationals who have been detained. Probably more than 2,500 people have been detained since September 11; their families and friends have reported them missing. Even now, I am not sure whether we know all their names, as the government will not confirm the identities of those in custody even to their attorneys. That is clearly interference with the individual's right to counsel.

Some regulatory changes made by Attorney General Ashcroft are even more alarming than the provisions of the USA Patriot Act. Many people are being detained on extremely technical immigration visa violations, and immigration judges will not release a person so long as the FBI expresses an interest in that individual. For example, in one case a student who forgot to sign an I-20 immigration form was picked up and has been in detention for six weeks. In its statement to the immigration court arguing to keep the

---

[7] Guantánamo Bay Naval Base, a U.S. facility located in eastern Cuba, is where the U.S. government has been holding and interrogating combatants captured in the Afghanistan war.

[8] Laura Murphy, summary of testimony before the District of Columbia, Maryland, and Virginia Advisory Committees to the U.S. Commission on Civil Rights, community forum, Annandale, Virginia, April 24–25, 2002, transcript, pp. 183–90, 224, 227–29, 232–34 (hereafter cited as Forum Transcript).

young man in custody, the FBI says it has been "unable to rule out" the possibility that he is somehow linked to or possesses knowledge of the terrorist attacks. If that doesn't suggest to you that people are being assumed guilty until proven innocent, I don't know what will. There is absolutely no allegation of any concrete fact that would relate this student in any way to the events of September 11.

In other cases, students fall out of status when they transfer schools and the paperwork is not done properly. People are being picked up on technical traffic violations as well. Bonds are being set very inconsistently.

I'm not as concerned about singling out young men from the Middle East for extra scrutiny at airports, but I am concerned about the large net cast by the so-called voluntary interviews, and about holding people in custody on technical visa violations. This is only being done to people who are Arab or Muslim—profiling of the worst sort.

Immigration proceedings are being conducted behind closed doors, closed to the public, with no reason given.[9] The attorney general also has promulgated a new regulation that says detention facilities cannot release any information about the detainees—who they are or where they are being held. Some people are being held on material witness warrants with no evidence that they know anything about September 11. Also, people are being shuttled back and forth, from a material witness warrant to criminal charges to an INS warrant, in order to keep them in detention. Judges are reluctant to release someone when the government says it has classified evidence that the person is a threat to national security, even though no evidence is presented.

The attorney general is asking people to come forward for voluntary interviews with the FBI and then, when they do, arresting them for minor visa violations or charging them with lying.[10]

---

[9] Attorney General Ashcroft has instituted new procedures for designated cases in immigration court, that is, those believed to be related to national security. These procedures require judges to hold the hearings individually, close the hearings to the public, and avoid disclosing any information about the cases to anyone outside the immigration court. Memorandum from Chief Immigration Judge Michael J. Creppy to all immigration judges and court administrators, "Cases Requiring Special Procedures," Sept. 21, 2001.

[10] Under 18 U.S.C. § 1001 it is a crime to make material false statements to a federal investigative agency.

That doesn't encourage voluntary compliance. Some of the supposed false statements may actually be due to misunderstandings or translation problems.

As an Arab American I recognize that the government has an obligation to protect us after what happened on September 11, and that task isn't easy for government officials. But the attacks had super devastating consequences for the Arab and Muslim communities in the United States, including people who are lawful permanent residents and U.S. citizens. All of us want to see the people responsible for September 11 brought to justice, but the government is implicating every single person of Arab or Muslim origin or belief, treating them as guilty unless they can prove themselves innocent. That is absolutely contrary to the American system of justice and the United States Constitution.[11]

Kelli M. Evans
Civil rights attorney, Rehlman Associates

My firm is currently representing four individuals who were removed from flights following September 11, not for any legitimate security reasons, but because of their Arab appearance.

In order to be effective, an airline security system must avoid bias and stereotyping. Bias may cause you either to read too much into innocent behavior or, alternatively, to ignore behavior that is objectively suspicious. Bias may explain why Richard Reid, a non-Arab man with explosive devices protruding from his shoes, was allowed to board a plane despite his erratic behavior and unusual travel patterns, while law-abiding individuals have been removed from flights.

Airline discrimination is not as bad as hate crimes or detentions, but it is more widespread and is feared by millions of law-abiding Americans who want to travel by air. We've fielded calls from Americans of all backgrounds who have been discriminated against by airlines since September 11 because they appear to be Arab. Some were not allowed to travel solely because airline employees or passengers were uncomfortable having them on board. Some were moved to seats in the back of the plane. In some cases, they were detained by law enforcement.

---

[11] Summary of testimony by Malea Kiblan, Forum Transcript, pp. 190–99, 225–27, 261–69.

Discrimination has a chilling effect on entire communities. It does not make us safer because a security profile that relies on race or ethnicity casts too wide a net and distracts attention from more accurate predictors, such as travel patterns and behavior.

Some people have suggested that Federal Aviation Administration (FAA) regulations permit the pilot to bar someone from a plane for any reason, but this is incorrect. Various laws and regulations prohibit airlines and their employees from discriminating against individuals on the basis of race, ethnicity, national origin, or religion. These laws include 42 U.S.C. § 1981 (1994), which prohibits racial discrimination in contracts and has been held to apply to airline discrimination, as well as numerous specific laws relating to air travel.

The U.S. Department of Transportation has issued fact sheets since September 11 clearly stating that singling out Arab, Middle Eastern, South Asian, and Muslim people because of their ethnicity or religion is unlawful.[12] However, these laws are not being adhered to by the airline industry.

There is a continuing lack of standardized security policies, procedures, and training for airline pilots and flight crews. Because of this, there are as many different airline security systems as there are planes in our skies. After September 11 Congress passed the Aviation and Transportation Security Act, directing the FAA in consultation with the new Transportation Security Administration (TSA) to give airlines detailed guidance, and requiring the airlines to develop programs to train their employees in security procedures.[13] It is essential that these new security policies and procedures address civil rights concerns. The government should require the airlines to develop written policies for how they will do this.

In sum, the Department of Transportation has unequivocally confirmed that discrimination based on race, ethnicity, national origin, and religion is illegal, but the airlines have failed to convert this guidance into operational policy and procedure. The FAA and the TSA should ensure that the airlines train their pilots and flight crews on these policies. We can and must make air travel safer without compromising America's values of equality and fair treatment.[14]

Raj Purohit
Legislative counsel, Washington office,
Lawyers Committee for Human Rights

In the months after September 11, more than 1,100 people were detained, mostly Arab and Muslim men. The authorities have refused to disclose their identities and places of detention, leaving families and advocates to struggle for information about those still in custody, as well as about the many who have been deported. As of April 12, 2002, more than 300 remain in custody. The majority of the detainees were held on immigration violations, primarily visa overstays, which the INS would not have prosecuted before last September.

Even in the face of the devastating terrorist attacks, there has been opposition both inside and outside the government to proposals to curtail civil rights, which has lessened the negative content of some of these measures.

The USA Patriot Act grants unprecedented new powers to the attorney general to detain noncitizens whom he certifies as a threat to national security, with minimal judicial review or due process safeguards. Civil rights organizations did succeed in adding a number of limitations to the bill. For example, the attorney general's certification of someone as a security threat is subject to judicial review, which may be sought in any federal district court. After seven days of detention, the government must either charge a detainee with a crime, initiate deportation, or release the person. The certification of a person as a suspected terrorist must be reviewed by a federal court every six months and either renewed or revoked. However, even these safeguards do not provide adequate protection against arbitrary detention. For instance, the seven-day limit on detention without charge is longer than the standard required by international law. And after the seven-day period, the

---

[12] *See* U.S. Department of Transportation, Federal Aviation Administration, "Guidance for Screeners and Other Security Personnel," <http://www.faa.gov/acr/Screeners.doc> (Oct. 27, 2002).

[13] The Aviation and Transportation Security Act, Pub. L. No. 107-71, 115 Stat. 597, was signed into law on November 19, 2001, and created the Transportation Security Administration, among other provisions.

[14] Summary of written testimony by Kelli Evans, read into the record by Chester Wickwire, Forum Transcript, pp. 199–207.

risk of detention and deportation remains for those ordered deported but who in practice cannot be returned to their home countries.

A key concern is the evidentiary threshold for certifying someone as a threat to national security. There are disturbing indications that the attorney general can rely heavily on secret evidence in making such determinations, which will be impossible to challenge in a review procedure. The law provides no guidance to the attorney general on procedures to follow in certifying someone as a suspected terrorist, nor to the courts regarding evidence they should consider in reviewing the certification.

While authority for long-term detentions was one of the most controversial issues in the debate on the USA Patriot Act, even before the law's adoption the government was already using new immigration regulations to detain noncitizens. New INS regulations issued in September 2001 allow noncitizens to be held without charge for 48 hours and longer in the event of extraordinary circumstances, which are left undefined.[15] These INS regulations go well beyond the provisions of the USA Patriot Act. This is one of the most troubling aspects of the investigation by DOJ. Detainees are being held on immigration violations but interrogated by the FBI about criminal-related matters; yet because they have not been charged criminally, they have no right to a lawyer.

There should be public discussion about critical issues such as how many people are in custody and for how long; have the detainees been certified as terrorists; what is the basis for the long-term detention of individuals without charge; and what is the reason for prolonged detention even after a deportation order has been granted.[16]

Paul K. Martin
Counselor, Office of the Inspector General, and acting special counsel for civil rights/civil liberties, Department of Justice

The Office of the Inspector General investigates complaints of civil rights or civil liberties abuses by U.S. Department of Justice employees, including those in the FBI, the INS, the Bureau of Prisons, and others. It is an independent entity within the Justice Department that reports both to the attorney general and to Congress. The USA Patriot Act, Section 1001, directs the Office of the Inspector General to (a) receive and review complaints of civil rights or civil liberties abuses by DOJ employees; (b) advertise on the Internet and through the media to let the public know how to file a complaint; and (c) report to Congress twice a year on implementation of this particular section of the act.[17] The Patriot legislation did not expand the authority of the Office of the Inspector General; we've always had the responsibility to investigate civil rights or civil liberties allegations. An earlier House of Representatives version of the bill contained much broader language that would have given the inspector general in the Justice Department wide responsibility for investigating ethnic and racial profiling as well, but these provisions were deleted from the final bill.

To date we have received about 350 complaints related to activities under the USA Patriot Act, but the majority deal with state or local agencies or other federal agencies, not with Justice Department employees. Currently we have seven open investigations, most dealing with allegations of physical abuse. They are potentially criminal cases, but if we cannot substantiate the criminal charges we'll pursue them as administrative cases. We have also received complaints about verbal abuse by correctional officers, discrimination by the INS, including racial profiling, rude treatment by INS inspectors, inmates not being permitted to practice the Muslim religion, detainees being held without access to attorneys, unlawful or warrantless searches, and detainees not being permitted to observe Ramadan while in INS custody.

In addition to investigating individual allegations, the Office of the Inspector General plans to conduct inspections or audits that examine systemic issues that we're seeing. Several weeks ago we initiated a review of the civil rights and civil liberties protections that were afforded to detainees in Department of Justice custody after September 11. Specifically, we're looking at federal detainees housed in the Passaic County jail in Paterson, New Jersey, and at the Metropoli-

---

[15] 8 C.F.R. § 287.3(d) (2001).

[16] Summary of testimony by Raj Purohit, Forum Transcript, pp. 208–17, 230–31.

[17] USA PATRIOT Act, Pub. L. No. 107-56, § 1001, 115 Stat. 272 at 391 (2001).

tan Detention Center in Brooklyn, New York. Our review will examine the detainees' right to counsel, the timeliness of presentation and disposition of charges, and physical detention conditions.

With respect to the advertising provisions in the act, we have conducted an active outreach program through the media to publicize the complaint procedure to potentially affected communities.[18]

Blane Workie
Trial attorney, Office of Aviation Enforcement and Proceedings, Office of the General Counsel, Department of Transportation

Three agencies within the Department of Transportation can receive complaints from members of the public who feel they've been discriminated against in air travel.[19] The newly created Transportation Security Administration handles complaints about the new federal security screeners. The Federal Aviation Administration investigates complaints against airport personnel, such as airport police. The Office of the General Counsel, which includes the Aviation Enforcement Office, receives complaints against air carrier personnel. We thoroughly investigate every complaint that we receive. However, we are statutorily limited in the remedies we can pursue.

Since September 11, we have received 30 complaints from persons alleging they were denied boarding or removed from aircraft because of their Arab, Middle Eastern, South Asian, Muslim, or Sikh appearance. We have also received 107 complaints of such discrimination by airlines prior to boarding. Most of the complaints were received before January 2002, so there has been a significant reduction in recent months.

The TSA is forming a federal security screening force whose preparation includes training in nondiscrimination. In addition to the screening at checkpoints, people can be selected at the ticket counter for additional security by CAPS, the computer assisted passenger screening system. The computer makes the selection based on predetermined criteria, which takes the subjectivity out of it.

Congress has mandated by statute that the new federal screeners hired and trained by the TSA be U.S. citizens. I understand that there is pending litigation on this issue.[20]

The enforcement office has reminded the airlines that federal law prohibits them from discriminating against passengers on the basis of race, color, national origin, religion, sex, or ancestry. We have also asked the major airlines to provide us information on all instances in which someone was denied boarding or removed from a plane since September 11, so we can compare that with the number of complaints we've received. We have met with representatives of the affected communities to hear their concerns, and we have done outreach in public forums to let people know how to file complaints. We haven't probed for violations using testers wearing headscarves, but this is a good idea that should be considered. We have done this kind of testing for passengers with disabilities—I myself have been at an airport in a wheelchair, to see how disabled passengers are treated—but we have not done it with respect to head coverings. I definitely do think it's a possibility.

We maintain a database where each new complaint is entered. Public perceptions of delay in responding to complaints may reflect the complexity of certain investigations, in which we have to interview many parties and it may take months or longer to close a case. But we can al-

---

[18] Summary of testimony by Paul Martin, Forum Transcript, pp. 218–22, 256–57.

[19] *See* Department of Transportation, Aviation Consumer Protection Division, "Air Travel Civil Rights Problems: Where to File Complaints," Oct. 2, 2002, <http://airconsumer.ost.dot.gov/DiscrimComplaintsContacts.htm> (Oct. 24, 2002).

[20] The firing of noncitizens from their jobs as security screeners has been an issue of concern. Under the Aviation and Transportation Security Act, the new Transportation Security Administration was charged with replacing private screeners with federal employees at the nation's airports by November 19, 2002, a task that required hiring more than 44,000 people. The law requires the new screeners to be U.S. citizens, have a high school diploma or one year of experience as a screener, and speak English. As a result, thousands of experienced screeners who are not U.S. citizens lost their jobs. Some lawmakers have supported a change to allow legal U.S. residents to apply for TSA jobs ("Security Jobs, Not Job Security," *Washington Post,* Oct. 4, 2002). In November 2002, in a case that could have nationwide implications, a federal judge in Los Angeles ruled the ban on noncitizen screeners unconstitutional and issued a preliminary injunction allowing nine noncitizen screeners to apply for federal screener jobs. Sara Kehaulani Goo, "Agency Meets Deadline for Airport Screeners," *Washington Post,* Nov. 19, 2002.

ways advise complainants of the status of their case.[21]

Kathleen A. Connon
National external program manager, Office of Civil Rights, Federal Aviation Administration, Department of Transportation

The FAA Office of Civil Rights investigates complaints about airports and airport personnel. Airports receive federal monies, so they must abide by federal civil rights laws. Because the FAA has the power to withdraw grant monies, airports are usually quick to comply with whatever the FAA wants them to do.

There are currently only two complaints pending against airport employees for discrimination, and both airports are working with us to retrain their personnel. The reason there have been so few complaints coming to our office is that only a few of the personnel you see in airports, mainly airport police officers, are actually employees of the airport itself. The screeners at security checkpoints are not airport employees; until recently, they were employees of private security companies contracted by the airlines. Complaints about them go to the Aviation Enforcement Office within DOT.

We require airports to have a sign at each checkpoint advising travelers of their rights. We have also sent fact sheets identifying discriminatory practices to airports and required them to advise their employees of these practices.[22]

---

[21] Summary of testimony by Blane Workie, Forum Transcript, pp. 235–42, 247–54, 258–60.

[22] Summary of testimony by Kathleen Connon, Forum Transcript, pp. 242–49.

Chapter 6

Fears and Concerns of Affected, At-Risk Communities

Panel Four heard from representatives of groups specifically targeted by the post-September 11 backlash: Arabs, South Asians, Muslims (including African American Muslims and Muslim women), and Sikhs. They described the impact of the backlash on their communities, citing not only hate violence and discrimination but also police harassment and civil liberties violations. The panelists also offered suggestions for how local and federal agencies could best respond to the types of incidents that have occurred.

The upsurge in hate crimes and discrimination against the affected groups during 2001 has been well documented in published reports. In its annual survey of hate crimes reported by state and local law enforcement agencies, the FBI counted 481 attacks against people of Middle Eastern descent, Muslims, and South Asian Sikhs during 2001, up from just 28 in 2000.[1] Surveys conducted by several advocacy and human rights groups noted similar patterns. The American-Arab Anti-Discrimination Committee (ADC) confirmed more than 700 violent incidents targeting members of the affected groups during the first nine weeks after the September 11 attacks, and 165 more incidents during the first nine months of 2002.[2] The FBI and ADC both found that while violent crimes have tapered off in 2002, job and housing discrimination remain persistent problems. ADC received more than 80 complaints of discrimination in air travel and more than 800 complaints of employment discrimination during the 13 months following the attacks.

In the weeks following September 11, there were four murders across the country that were confirmed as hate related, and at least seven more suspected hate crime murders.[3] On September 15 in Mesa, Arizona, an Indian Sikh, Balbir Singh Sodhi, was shot and killed while planting flowers outside his gas station. Prosecutors have accused Frank Roque of going on a shooting rampage in which he first killed Sodhi, then fired on the home of an Afghan family, and finally shot at a Lebanese American gas station clerk. During his arrest Roque yelled statements such as "I am a patriot!" and "I stand for America all the way!" In the Dallas area, a white supremacist, Mark Anthony Stroman, killed two people: Waqar Hasan, a Pakistani Muslim, shot in the face on September 15 while cooking hamburgers in his grocery store; and Vasudev Patel, an Indian American, shot in the chest on October 4 while working with his wife behind the counter of a gas station they owned. Stroman told a Dallas radio station he killed Hasan and Patel to seek revenge for the World Trade Center attacks, "to retaliate on local Arab Americans or whatever you want to call them."[4] And on

---

[1] Federal Bureau of Investigation, Uniform Crime Reporting Program, "Hate Crime Statistics 2001," Nov. 25, 2002, <www.fbi.gov/ucr/o1hate.pdf> (Dec. 2, 2002).

[2] American-Arab Anti-Discrimination Committee (ADC) Research Institute, *Report on Hate Crimes and Discrimination Against Arab Americans September 11, 2001 to October 11, 2002* (available from Laila Al-Qatami at lalqatami@adc.org or (202) 244-2990). The FBI and the ADC used slightly different criteria to define and verify incidents; the ADC report includes incidents reported to the organization and to the news media as well as those reported to law enforcement.

[3] These examples and the examples in the following paragraphs are drawn from ADC Research Institute, *Report on Hate Crimes and Discrimination*, and press reports.

[4] Stroman was subsequently tried and convicted of Patel's murder. *See also* Robert E. Pierre, "Victims of Hate, Now Feeling Forgotten," *Washington Post*, Sept. 14, 2002.

September 19 in Lincoln Park, Michigan, Ali Almansoop, a U.S. citizen originally from Yemen, was shot in the back while fleeing his attacker, who threatened, "I'm going to kill you for what happened in New York and D.C."

In the Washington, D.C., metropolitan area, a number of physical assaults were reported. For example, in Falls Church, Virginia, on September 14, 2001, a motorist pulled alongside a delivery truck and asked the deliveryman his ethnicity. When the deliveryman responded "Afghan," the attacker threatened and pursued him. When the delivery truck pulled into a parking lot, the attacker approached the van and began punching the driver. Witnesses screamed for the attacker to stop, and one woman threw herself in between the two men. "Why are you telling me to leave? Why didn't you tell him to leave? This is my country. You should tell him to leave," the attacker shouted.[5]

Some assaults and hate speech specifically targeted Muslim women, easily visible because of their headscarves. For example, on September 11, 2001, in Columbia, Maryland, a motorist stuck his head out of his car window and yelled to the next car at a Muslim woman wearing a *hijab,* "You better hide."[6] On September 28 in Falls Church, Virginia, an unknown attacker struck a Muslim woman in the head with a baseball bat. She struggled to get to the local mosque to take refuge. Although mosque officials urged her to contact the police, she refused, citing her uncertain immigration status.[7]

Local cases also included many attacks and threats against mosques and Islamic centers. In the days following September 11, hate messages were left on the answering machine of a mosque in Manassas, Virginia; the Dar Al Hijra Islamic Center in Falls Church, Virginia, received threats; and the Islamic Center in Washington, D.C., received bomb threats, forcing the closure of Massachusetts Avenue NW, where the center is located. In Sterling, Virginia, on September 12, local Muslim residents gathered at their worship center to go by chartered bus to a Red Cross center to donate blood. At their worship center,

they found their hallway spray painted in thick black letters, several feet tall, spelling out "Die Pigs" and "Muslims Burn Forever."[8]

Businesses and homes owned by people from the affected groups were targeted. In Rockville, Maryland, a rug company owned by a Palestinian immigrant was set on fire. An Afghan restaurant in Washington, D.C., was struck by vandals who broke the front window and wrote threatening graffiti on the storefront, including a message saying, "You guys destroy my country, we have to destroy you."[9] In Alexandria, Virginia, windows were broken at an Islamic bookstore. The owner found two bricks on the premises with notes that said, "You come to this country and kill. You must die as well," and "Arab murderers." A local businessman donated his time and resources to repair the windows.[10] And on September 27, 2001, in Fairfax, Virginia, a large swastika was burned into the front lawn of a Middle Eastern family's home.[11]

Many cases of employment discrimination were reported in the local area after September 11. To cite just a few examples, on September 15 an Arab American was fired from his position as a strategy consultant with an Arlington, Virginia, firm. The company claimed that his termination was due to a reduction in the workforce. However, before September 11 he had been the first person placed on a consultancy team because his performance had been exceptional, and he was more qualified than his colleagues who remained on the team. In Washington, D.C., an Afghan janitor at a restaurant faced harassment from the restaurant's chef, who nicknamed him "Taliban" and spoke to him in offensive tones. The janitor was stripped of his working hours and finally was fired for allegedly arguing with the restaurant's manager. In Gaithersburg, Maryland, an Arab American construction worker faced constant threats with vulgar language at work. A co-worker acted as though he would attack him with a metal pipe. When he reported the threats and hostility, his

---

[5] ADC Research Institute, *Report on Hate Crimes,* citing the *Washington Post.*

[6] ADC Research Institute, *Report on Hate Crimes,* citing the *Baltimore Sun,* Sept. 14, 2001.

[7] ADC Research Institute, *Report on Hate Crimes,* citing the *Washington Post,* Sept. 23, 2001.

[8] ADC Research Institute, *Report on Hate Crimes,* citing the *Washington Post,* Sept. 13, 2001.

[9] ADC Research Institute, *Report on Hate Crimes,* citing the *Washington Times,* Feb. 11, 2002.

[10] Ibid.

[11] ADC Research Institute, *Report on Hate Crimes,* citing the *Washington Post,* Oct. 11, 2001.

supervisor responded with, "Well, don't you think they have a right to be angry?"

Incidents of discrimination in air travel occurred at the three area airports. In some cases, individuals were denied boarding or removed from aircraft after they had already passed through security screening. An Arab American traveler at Baltimore/Washington International Airport on October 31, 2001, was boarding a flight after having passed through regular security screening. While in the gateway leading to the plane, he looked at a woman next to him and politely insisted, "Go ahead ma'am," giving her permission to walk in front of him. She responded with a dirty look and did not move. Shortly thereafter he turned to see her talking to a security agent. The agent approached the Arab American traveler minutes later in the plane and directed him to get off the flight. He was told that the woman had reported that he had been "acting strange." He was then scheduled for a later flight. Complaints were also received of travelers being required to remove religiously mandated head coverings—Muslim women's scarves and Sikh turbans—at screening checkpoints even though the metal detector did not sound.

In one typical example, on December 18, 2001, at Baltimore/Washington International Airport a 17-year-old Muslim high school student from Virginia was passing through security when she was stopped by an airport security guard. "Hey, you need to take that off," the guard called out, referring to her *hijab*. "Why do I have to take off my head cover?" the girl asked, when suddenly nearby military personnel approached her. The sight of the guards in camouflage and carrying combat rifles intimidated the teenager and she quickly took off her scarf. A Muslim airport employee informed the guard that it was wrong to force the student to remove her headscarf in public.[12]

Another type of discrimination involved harassment of individuals by police on the basis of their appearance. On October 8, 2001, in Alexandria, Virginia, an Arab American motorist and his two Arab passengers were stopped by two city police officers who asked about the verse of the Quran hanging from the car's rearview mirror. One of the officers inquired about docu-

ments and photocopies in the backseat. After asking for everyone's identification cards, he was granted permission to search the car. He took one passenger's identification card and the driver's license, returned to his car, and drove off without explanation. The Arab American motorist called 911. About 10 minutes later the officer returned and said that he had received a call and had to leave. According to the driver, the officer did not have his siren or lights on when he drove away.

Referencing many of these same types of incidents, the panelists at the forum made several major points:

- Their communities, which are solidly part of American society, condemned the September 11 attacks and want to see the perpetrators brought to justice.

- Members of these communities have suffered unprecedented levels of hate violence, threats, and harassment, as well as discrimination in air travel, employment, housing, education, and other areas since September 11.

- The lack of vigorous federal agency response is of concern to the affected communities. Although some government agencies have been receptive to individual complaints of civil rights violations, and federal officials in meetings give the impression that they care about these concerns, they typically fail to follow through with action.

- While incidents of hate violence have gradually tapered off in the year since September 11, concerns have grown about civil liberties violations; indeed, some of the affected groups now see threats to civil liberties as the main worry, overshadowing hate violence. Racial profiling, searches, interrogations, detentions, and, most recently, the raids by federal agents in Northern Virginia have violated people's civil rights and led to deep distrust of the authorities among members of the affected communities.

- The federal government has asked for help from Muslims and Arab Americans in identifying potential terrorist threats, but at the same time it is alienating those communities through aggressive violations of their civil rights.

---

[12] ADC Research Institute, *Report on Hate Crimes,* citing Council on American-Islamic Relations, Jan. 8, 2002.

Johari Abdul-Malik
Muslim chaplain, Howard University

According to some estimates, African Americans make up about a third of all Muslims in the United States, and 84 percent of new converts to Islam. The majority of African American Muslims in this country are Sunni Muslims; a small minority belong to the Nation of Islam.[13]

African American Muslims are punished in two ways: on one hand they're perceived as disloyal Americans because they had the audacity to select a "foreign" religion, and on the other hand they're mistaken for foreigners because of their name or appearance, especially in the case of women who wear headscarves. American Muslim women are seen from afar and the evaluation is, well, they're brown, they're wearing some foreign-type dress that looks Islamic, and therefore this person is not a citizen. An American Muslim woman will go to work and someone will yell to her, "Why don't you go back home?" And she says, "I'm from Herndon."

Since September 11, we are getting reports of discrimination against Muslims in the workplace. In some cases, when Arab American Muslims face workplace discrimination they will go to an African American Muslim co-worker and ask him or her to speak up on their behalf. Then the African American Muslim also becomes the target of workplace discrimination. We are also getting reports of Muslims being discriminated against in housing applications and in hiring. Children are being taunted in public schools—"Osama bin Laden, why don't you go back to where you came from?"—even though most were born here. Muslims are heckled in public, or warned of the risk they run by wearing head coverings. Hate crimes have affected all segments of the Muslim community.

We are getting reports now of Muslims being discriminated against in housing applications and in hiring. Applicants are asked, "Are you a Muslim?"—and then don't get a call back. One young man in the information technology field told me he had a great résumé but never got calls back. So he changed his name from Khalid to Ted and was hired in a week.

The community is very much concerned about the detentions and the working links between the INS and the FBI. We have been encouraging our community to cooperate with law enforcement, but when they do, it turns to coercion based on immigration status. Agents ask, "You're African American, you go to such-and-such a mosque, do you know so-and-so?" And you know the outcome is going to be that the INS and FBI walk in together, and that a person who was going to cooperate is now coerced to cooperate because one of his friends or relatives is out of status.

Prominent Islamic institutions in Northern Virginia were the victims first of vandalism, then of raids by law enforcement agents. So far there have been no indictments and no arrests. These are upstanding members of our communities.[14]

Kareem W. Shora
Legal advisor, American-Arab Anti-Discrimination Committee

Since September 11, the Arab American community has experienced an unprecedented backlash in the form of hate crimes, various forms of discrimination, and serious civil liberties concerns. The American-Arab Anti-Discrimination Committee has compiled reports of more than 600 violent incidents directed against Arab Americans and people perceived to be Arab, including Sikhs, South Asians, and Latinos.[15] These incidents include acts of physical violence such as vandalism, arson, beatings, and assault with weapons; also included are threats of violence, such as bomb threats and hostile phone calls.[16]

---

[13] Although Louis Farrakhan agreed in 2000 to adopt the general tenets of worldwide Islam, the Nation of Islam maintains a separate organizational structure and has remained somewhat isolated, according to Mr. Abdul-Malik.

[14] Johari Abdul-Malik, summary of testimony before the District of Columbia, Maryland, and Virginia Advisory Committees to the U.S. Commission on Civil Rights, community forum, Annandale, Virginia, April 24–25, 2002, transcript, pp. 309–16, 364–65, 371, 411 (hereafter cited as Forum Transcript).

[15] More than 700 violent incidents targeting Arab Americans or those perceived to be Arab Americans, Arabs, and Muslims in the first nine weeks following September 11, 2001, were reported by the American-Arab Anti-Discrimination Committee Research Institute in its report titled *Report on Hate Crimes & Discrimination Against Arab Americans: The Post-September 11 Backlash*, May 2003. Copies may be obtained by e-mailing adc@adc.org or calling (202) 244-2990.

[16] The incidents are summarized in ADC Research Institute, *Report on Hate Crimes*. The final version of the report covered the period up to October 11, 2002, and thus contained a

Airline racism is a major issue. ADC has confirmed more than 60 cases in which passengers who were perceived to be Arab have been expelled from planes because passengers or crew members do not like the way they look or don't feel safe with them on board. Federal agencies, specifically the U.S. Department of Transportation and the FAA, have done a good job of communicating the official view that this is unacceptable, but there is a lack of enforcement and these incidents are still happening. We're getting words, but not actions.

Workplace and employment discrimination have grown tremendously since September 11, and ADC has confirmed 230 such incidents. All were reported to the Equal Employment Opportunity Commission, which has done an outstanding job of responding to the Arab American community and indeed has probably been the federal agency most responsive to our concerns. For example, they have created a special code—Code "Z"—to address complaints that may be related to the backlash against Arabs and Muslims. Virginia is one of the top six states in terms of the number of reported employment discrimination cases since September 11.

Another concern is law enforcement profiling. ADC has received dozens of reports of Arab Americans or those mistaken for Arab Americans being searched and questioned by local police for no apparent reason. In one typical example, an Arab American motorist was stopped and searched by Alexandria, Virginia, police solely because he had a small version of the Quran hanging from his rearview mirror. This and many other incidents were reported to the Civil Rights Division of the U.S. Department of Justice, which has created a special task force.

Other problems include violent harassment in schools and universities (45 cases confirmed) and denial of service, such as in restaurants (23 cases confirmed).

The major area of concern now, however, is threats to civil liberties. Arab Americans are becoming afraid of the federal government, mainly because of actions by the Justice Department. The community was shaken by the March 20 raids in Northern Virginia carried out by a task force of the U.S. Treasury Department and other law enforcement and customs officials.

ADC objects to the secrecy and the way in which these raids were conducted. The people targeted were stable and respected members of the community. Agents could have knocked on their doors and been invited in. Instead the agents smashed down doors, yelling and screaming, handcuffed people, and seized personal property, much of which has not been returned. And nobody has been charged with any crime.

We are also very concerned about the interviews being conducted by the Justice Department using U.S. attorneys' offices as well as FBI field offices. The attorney general said these would be voluntary interviews of 5,000 Arab men with nonimmigrant visas, but many U.S. citizens, including some born here, have also been summoned for questioning. The answers given in the interviews are being compiled in a federal database. This creates fear and hostility toward the federal government. When you do this to a community that you're looking for help from, you're basically not going to get that help.

While the government makes statements against racial profiling, rumors fly through the Arab American community about the latest detentions. People are getting conflicting messages from the government. For example, the DOJ Civil Rights Division is doing a good job of outreach, but other elements within DOJ, including the leadership, send a very different message.

There is a lot of negativity in the media. Self-proclaimed terrorism experts go on TV, claiming to be experts on Arabs and Islam, when in fact they've never been to any Arab country and just spout stereotypes. They get Ph.Ds in psychology and political science and decide to write a book on terrorism, and all of a sudden they're on CNN and MSNBC giving you their opinions every night on prime time. It is no help whatsoever. If you want experts, you should talk to people from within the community. If you want to understand Islam, talk to an imam. If you want to understand something about Arab culture, talk to an Arab American. They'll tell you both the positives and the negatives rather than the stereotypical rhetoric that's on TV almost every night.[17]

---

higher number of incidents in every category than the figures mentioned by Mr. Shora at the April forum.

[17] Summary of testimony by Kareem Shora, Forum Transcript, pp. 317–24, 385–89, 394–95, 408–09.

Rajwant Singh
President, Sikh Council on Religion and Education

Americans have little information about the Sikh religion. The religion was founded on the principles of equality of all persons regardless of gender, race, religion, caste, or social status. Sikhs are identified by their distinctive dress, which includes uncut hair, beard, turban, and a small ceremonial sword, or *kirpan*. To a Sikh, the turban protects the uncut hair and is a symbol of his spiritual identity and commitment to spiritual discipline as required by the founders of the faith. Sikhs have been part of this country since the beginning of the last century and contribute to American society in many different fields.

The Sikh community has faced severe problems in the aftermath of the September 11 tragedies.[18] Our very distinctive appearance has made us the targets of hate, as Americans wrongly assume we are associated with terrorists. Hate crimes and incidents against Sikhs have increased dramatically since September 11. More than 300 hate crimes and incidents against Sikhs have been reported since that date, ranging from verbal abuse to physical assault and even murder. A Sikh gas station owner was shot and killed on September 15, 2001, in Mesa, Arizona, by someone who said he looked like Osama bin Laden.[19] Other examples include a child hit with a bottle of flammable material in California, an arson attempt on a Sikh worship place in Cleveland, vandalism of worship places in California and homes in Virginia and Colorado, an assault with a baseball bat on an elderly man in New York, arson against a Sikh-owned convenience store in New York, an assault on a middle school student, and many others. Sikhs have had garbage and eggs thrown at them, have had guns shown to them, and have been shoved and pushed.

The Sikh community is enduring profiling at an unprecedented level, with people singled out for searches and questioning by federal, state, and local law enforcement and by airport screeners. These include turban searches. On September 12, 2001, Sher Singh of Leesburg, Virginia, was taken off an Amtrak train by police in Providence, Rhode Island, searched, and taken into custody because he carried a *kirpan*, a ceremonial knife less than four inches long. His picture with handcuffs was shown repeatedly by the national and international media, even after the charges were dropped, as a suspect that had been apprehended. We believe this publicity contributed to the subsequent murder of the Sikh in Mesa, Arizona.

Young Sikhs in schools and colleges have endured verbal and physical assaults. We also face increasing hostility in the workplace, with Sikh employees being required to cut their hair and remove their turbans in order to keep their jobs. For example, a few weeks after September 11 a Sikh American working for a shipping service delivered a package to a business as part of his job. A person who saw the Sikh leaving the building called the local police, saying that a person with a turban who looked Arab had delivered a suspicious package to the business. The police evacuated the building, fearing that a bomb was in the package. After hearing of the incident, the Sikh courier's manager said that there had been customer complaints about his appearance and asked him to remove his turban and cut his beard. In fear of losing his livelihood, the Sikh American reluctantly complied. He trimmed his beard and replaced his turban with a baseball cap. He was fired anyway and has since had difficulty finding a job. We have talked to the family and the gentleman. He is severely depressed because of this incident.

These problems stem from ignorance of our culture. Ninety-nine percent of the people in this country who wear turbans are Sikhs, yet we are seen as somehow related to Osama bin Laden. We have advised our people not to shave their beards or remove their turbans. Rather, we are trying to educate outsiders about us, a tremendous task.

Our community believes that laws against hate crimes should be enforced. There should be legislation to regulate airport searches, including turban searches, with fines for arbitrary actions by airport security personnel. The government should create fact sheets on groups affected by the backlash after September 11 and increase outreach to these communities. Efforts are needed to raise awareness of the Sikh community and other affected communities, includ-

---

[18] Many press articles documenting the backlash against Sikh Americans can be found at <www.attacksonsikhs.com>.

[19] Mr. Singh later added that the Department of Justice has not moved ahead on prosecution of the murder of Balbir Singh Sodhi. Although it is being prosecuted locally as a homicide, he stated, it should also be dealt with at the federal level as a hate crime. Forum Transcript, p. 391.

ing images of Sikhs as Americans in the media. Training should be provided to federal, state, and local agencies to raise awareness of who Sikhs are, and steps should be taken to incorporate cultural awareness in curricula and inform teachers and school administrators about the affected communities. And finally, we should hold events that encourage members of different religious and ethnic communities to learn about each other.[20]

Sharifa Alkhateeb

President, North American Council for Muslim Women

We share the nation's sorrow over the tragic events of September 11 and wish to see the perpetrators brought to justice.

Many hate crimes after September 11 were directed specifically at Muslim women, and forced them to make very uncomfortable decisions about their freedom of movement, speech, and dress, for fear of their safety in public and even in their own homes. Most Muslim women in America felt very intimidated and frightened in the early weeks after the attacks, and continue to feel so today. Many Muslim women continue to receive hate messages by mail and e-mail, such as the widely circulated statement, "Put a match to every scarf-head." Even today, women are being subjected to cursing, spitting, screaming, staring menacingly, being poked or punched, teasing, name-calling, being pushed, cars following them and sometimes bumping their cars, strangers giving them the finger or yelling at them to go back home. I have personally experienced almost all of these. One such incident was in downtown Washington, D.C., on M Street: a man rolled down his window and screamed curses at me, for no reason at all. Muslim children in public schools were also subjected to all the behaviors mentioned above; in a few instances, the person taunting them was their own teacher or their principal.

After September 11, some religious and community leaders advised Muslim women to remove their head coverings or even stay at home. Some did for a while, and some also withdrew their children from school. Many good non-Muslim neighbors helped by offering to escort Muslim women when they needed to go out.

Some non-Muslim women even put on head-scarves on designated days to show solidarity with Muslim women.

The media in this country took an extremely negative attitude toward anyone Muslim and anything "Islamic," with one anti-Arab, anti-Muslim barrage or diatribe after another. This has resulted in Muslim women feeling judged by all to be guilty of something at all times. The number one fear of Muslim women in America today is being treated unfairly by those who do not know them. If they wear a head covering, they fear some stranger pulling it off or doing them some bodily harm.

These fears were made more concrete as a result of the recent raids here in the Herndon, Virginia, area. Agents appeared at homes, businesses, and schools shouting and banging on doors, armed with machine guns and bulletproof vests. They showed identification to some and to others they did not; in some cases they did not show any warrant but just entered and proceeded to search. Some doors were broken down. The authorities ran through premises looking for anyone who was not a U.S. citizen. In some instances, they treated people very badly until they saw their U.S. passports. Some investigators participating in the raids became very angry and verbally violent when questioned about anything at all that had to do with the search. Two women and one teenage boy were handcuffed for several hours. Two Muslim women who wear head coverings normally were not wearing them when the government agents came in and they refused to allow the women to put on their religiously mandated head coverings for several hours. They took every computer from the premises as well as boxes of papers, money and other valuables, and even people's personal diaries. In at least one case, agents left the entire home in complete disarray. News of this went out very quickly and traumatized Muslim women all over the country.

We met with Treasury Secretary Paul O'Neill and asked for information about the protocol for how the raids were conducted, but his office never provided the information and did not respond to follow-up calls. They call meetings to give the impression that they care about your

---

[20] Summary of testimony by Rajwant Singh, Forum Transcript, pp. 325–33, 391–92, 410–11.

concerns, but they don't do anything about them.[21]

For every complaint that is filed, another 10 are never brought forward because people are scared to death of being taken away if they speak up.[22] Our organization has been organizing town meetings in our communities with representatives of federal agencies, which have helped somewhat to convince people that the government is not out to get every Arab and Muslim.

Some good things have happened as a result of the backlash. For example, four mosques in Fairfax County, Virginia, received government grants to provide counseling and other services to the Muslim community. This was a vote of confidence in the Muslim community by the county and the government. Additionally, although the media coverage has been heavily anti-Arab and anti-Muslim, it nonetheless has served to increase the average American's interest in learning more about these groups. Since September 11, our organization has participated in more than 200 events, including interfaith dialogues, meetings with public officials, media appearances, and teach-ins at universities, churches, and other institutions.

Our recommendations:

- Legal penalties for hate crimes should be publicized.

- Police should come to the scene when people report an abuse.

- There should be publicity regarding how to file complaints of civil rights violations.

- The White House should be advised of the potential consequences of public statements they make—such as Attorney General Ashcroft's statement that funds would be given to neighborhood watch groups to spy on Muslim and Arab neighbors.

- Relief monies intended for the Muslim American community should be channeled through Muslim groups.[23]

Gautam Dutta

Vice president, South Asian Bar Association

South Asia is a very large and diverse subcontinent, with many religions, and South Asian immigrants to the United States reflect that diversity. They include Hindus, Muslims, Buddhists, Sikhs, and even Christians and Jews.

The nonprofit organization South Asian American Leaders of Tomorrow compiled a report on the violent attacks against South Asians, Arabs, Muslims, and Sikhs in the first week after September 11.[24] The report documents 645 reported hate crime incidents during September 11–17, including three killings of South Asians as well as several killings of Arab Americans. The violence has touched many different communities, including Latinos—anyone who resembles what people think a terrorist should look like is at risk. There were also at least 49 assaults and 92 incidents of vandalism or arson, and 465 incidents of threats and intimidation. A lawyer colleague of mine was chased down the streets of Manhattan on September 12, 2001. Another colleague of mine was kicked off an airplane just because he looked South Asian. As for me personally, I was walking down the street with some South Asian friends two or three weeks after September 11 and a passerby said, "Your people must be really happy about the attacks." I don't know which people he's talking about. We're all Americans, too.

The South Asian community has always been treated as "foreign." The community experienced many violent attacks even before September 11, but a lot of South Asians believed that as long as they work hard and contribute to society, no one will harm them. Suddenly, people are realizing that they are vulnerable.

There is now widespread concern about racial profiling and discrimination: being pulled off airplanes, being pulled over just because you look Sikh. There's concern about the detentions

[21] Consistent with this, a member of the audience, June Han of the National Asian Pacific American Legal Consortium, remarked that initial outreach by federal agencies to vulnerable communities has been good and they have shown openness to receiving complaints; the problem is lack of follow-up. She suggested the need for a formal follow-up mechanism. Forum Transcript, pp. 405–06.

[22] Albert Mokaiber, an Arab American attorney in the forum audience, said, "We go to the Department of Justice and we're told all the right things about civil rights, and no sooner do we leave than there's somebody behind us following us all the way back." Forum Transcript, p. 400.

[23] Summary of testimony by Sharifa Alkhateeb, Forum Transcript, pp. 334–45, 372–73, 384–85, 401, 409–10.

[24] South Asian American Leaders of Tomorrow, *American Backlash*, Sept. 28, 2001, <www.saalt.org/abr.htm> (Oct. 27, 2002).

of many South Asians by the federal government right now. And in a broader sense, there's concern about whether South Asians will ever be accepted as Americans. South Asians now have more empathy for groups that have suffered from racial profiling in the past—African Americans, Latinos. We're all in the same boat and we have to fight for our rights.

There are mixed messages coming from the government, so top political leaders need to make clear statements about hate crimes. They should get the word out that hate crimes will not be tolerated and let people know what to do if they are affected. At present, there is often reluctance to go to the authorities because of fear and embarrassment. At the same time, local and state governments must get over their denial that hate crimes do occur.

We, members of affected groups, all need to be more proactive in working to promote understanding. People need to see that we are not the "Other."[25]

Joseph Zogby
Special counsel for post-September 11 national origin discrimination, Civil Rights Division, Department of Justice

Since September 11, we have seen a substantial increase in reported bias incidents against Arab Americans, Muslim Americans, South Asian Americans, and Sikh Americans, as well as others perceived to be members of these groups. These incidents include hate crimes and discrimination in employment, housing, education, public accommodations, and air travel. The Department of Justice is taking this problem very seriously and is devoting significant resources to it.

The Civil Rights Division reacted swiftly to stem the backlash, issuing a statement on September 13, 2001, that threats of violence or discrimination against these groups are wrong, un-American, and unlawful. We met with representatives of the affected communities on the same day, and have continued to meet with them. We also created a post-September 11 initiative within the Civil Rights Division's National Origin Working Group. This initiative seeks to combat discrimination in three ways. First, we receive reports of violations, maintain a database of complaints, and refer complaints to the proper federal agencies. Second, we do outreach to vulnerable communities, working with Arab, Sikh, and Muslim community organizations to enable people to file complaints. This has included holding community forums in Arlington, Virginia, and several other locations. Third, we work with other DOJ components and with other government agencies to provide interagency coordination to address the backlash.

With the help of the FBI, the U.S. attorneys' offices, and local prosecutors, the Civil Rights Division has opened more than 350 criminal investigations into alleged hate crimes, including telephone, Internet, mail, and face-to-face threats; minor assaults; assaults with dangerous weapons; assaults resulting in serious injury or death; and vandalism, shootings, and bombings aimed at homes, businesses, and places of worship. We also have dozens of civil investigations under way into alleged noncriminal bias incidents.

The Civil Rights Division and the U.S. attorneys' offices continue to coordinate with local prosecutors to bring federal charges where appropriate. Federal charges have been brought in 10 cases so far. Additional prosecutions may take place in response to the 350 investigations opened since September 2001, but with each complaint a determination must be made whether it rises to the threshold of having violated federal civil rights law. In some cases, these crimes have to be prosecuted at the state and local level.

Regarding violations of civil rights by government personnel, there are two offices in the Justice Department charged with investigating allegations of abuses by the department's personnel and by state and local law enforcement. Complaints about the Operation Green Quest raids have been filed with the Customs Service of the Treasury Department, which is heading up that operation, and some investigations have been opened. Treasury Secretary O'Neill has also met with Arab American and Muslim leaders to discuss their concerns about the raids.[26]

---

[25] Summary of testimony by Gautam Dutta, Forum Transcript, pp. 345–53, 389, 412.

[26] Summary of testimony by Joseph Zogby, Forum Transcript, pp. 354–62, 366–70, 374–77, 379–82, 389–92, 399–400, 406–07.

Chapter 7

Local Government Responses and Best Practices

The final panel heard from representatives of local government agencies in the Washington, D.C., metropolitan area, mainly in Maryland and Virginia jurisdictions, who described some of the actions taken by their agencies on and after September 11, 2001, to respond to the emergency and ensure the safety of groups affected by the backlash.[1] In addition, a representative of the U.S. Justice Department's Community Relations Service spoke about this unit's efforts to assist local authorities across the country in meeting this challenge, and staff members of two Islamic educational organizations commented on the response by schools and law enforcement. Among the major points made by the Panel Five speakers:

- Efforts to promote understanding between different ethnic and religious groups in communities and in schools began in many cases well before September 11, and these efforts provided a firm foundation for the post-September 11 response.

- Immediately after the terrorist attacks, local authorities began proactive outreach to vulnerable groups and took steps to protect them from a backlash; these efforts continued for

some weeks afterward, even as local law enforcement was monitoring a spike in hate crimes.

- In the months since the attacks, many positive programs have been initiated in school systems and communities aimed at bringing people together and building understanding and tolerance.

- The Justice Department's movement toward empowering local police forces to enforce federal immigration laws threatens to destroy the trust that local police are working to build in their communities.

Ronald Clarkson
Community relations manager, Office of the County Executive, Montgomery County, Maryland

The situation in the beginning was very tense and the atmosphere was one of disbelief. On the afternoon of September 11, we started making phone calls to representatives of the communities that we thought might experience retaliation, to find out what was happening and let them know we were available to help. The police department also started similar outreach, offering to do security checks at facilities, to give them the maximum protection possible and also let them know that the county does care. This was based on our own guess that people might retaliate for the terrorist attacks, because we know that in the past even lesser incidents have put gasoline on the fire in terms of people acting out their hatred.

We were active that entire week, going out to locations, talking to people, trying to reassure the community and make sure things were under control. The county executive organized an interfaith prayer service on September 14 and made a statement at that event calling for toler-

---

[1] Regrettably, no representative of the District of Columbia government attended the forum, despite a written invitation and follow-up calls to the mayor's office. The deputy mayor who agreed to attend the forum did not attend or send word, nor did the mayor's office respond to an invitation to provide a written statement after the event. The SAC members therefore were unable to learn about specific initiatives taken by the D.C. government, police, or schools to respond to the events of September 11. The forum did, however, hear from a member of the board of directors of the Metropolitan Washington Council of Governments, which includes the D.C. government.

ance and respect for differences. Since then, the county Human Rights Commission has visited mosques and other places in the community to discuss people's concerns. We mounted an education campaign around the anthrax threats, holding public forums to talk about bioterrorism preparedness and about tolerance. There were some minor hate incidents reported in the county, but no physical violence.

Every year in December the county executive holds an ecumenical prayer service. The December 2001 service, which fell during the month of Ramadan, was held in a mosque and drew the largest turnout we've ever had for one of our prayer services. It was an unspoken statement that we recognize the value of the mosque in the community, that we are going to learn as much as we can about the Muslim community, and make sure that we do not victimize that community.[2]

Charles Moose

Chief of police, Montgomery County, Maryland

Our police department's response to September 11 has been in three broad areas: community outreach, public safety coordination, and internal issues. As a result of September 11, many people in our community were identified right away as "culprits," and we had a tremendous spike in our hate crime statistics. Within hours of the attacks, the Montgomery County police department put squad cars at mosques and Jewish facilities in the county to protect them. Since then, we've done aggressive investigation of the spike in hate crimes and are working with affected communities to track trends and patterns so that they can assist us in finding solutions.

In public safety coordination, we have tried to pool our cultural and language resources as we respond. In terms of internal response, we reissued our policy and directive on civil and human rights. We've provided counseling for people in the community and inside the agency so the stress they feel doesn't manifest itself in violence.

We need to increase the diversity in the law enforcement workforce and make sure the workforce we have is knowledgeable and sensitive.

But certain groups don't seem to seek out public safety jobs. It is a challenge we continually face.

I am very concerned about the movement by the Department of Justice to ask local law enforcement to do immigration work.[3] When the FBI has asked local law enforcement to go with them to interview specific people, we did join them because it was in the context of specific questions about possible crimes. But we are not trained to enforce federal immigration laws. We've spent years trying to build trust with communities, and we have come a long way; asking us to do immigration work is a hand grenade to destroy all of that trust. It threatens to destroy all the progress we have made. It is clearly the wrong direction, but it's coming from the top down. It puts us in a precarious position and will force someone like myself to give thought to whether 27 years in law enforcement may be enough. I should note, though, that the law enforcement community is divided on this concept, and some leaders in law enforcement endorse it.

Regarding the proposal in certain states such as Virginia to identify immigration status on driver's licenses, this is foolishness that cannot solve the problem. Before September 11, the biggest terrorist act in America was committed by Timothy McVeigh, whose driver's license wouldn't have shown anything unusual.

There are two different approaches to solving this problem: the criminal justice approach and the "war" approach. With war, a lot of rules go out the window. Since September 11, people have been willing to throw some things out the

---

[2] Ronald Clarkson, summary of testimony before the District of Columbia, Maryland, and Virginia Advisory Committees to the U.S. Commission on Civil Rights, community forum, Annandale, Virginia, April 24–25, 2002, transcript, pp. 416–24, 505–07 (hereafter cited as Forum Transcript).

[3] Historically, only the U.S. Department of Justice has had authority to enforce federal immigration laws, but Attorney General Ashcroft is now moving to empower local law enforcement to make arrests on civil immigration violations as part of the war on terrorism. In 1996 Congress authorized the attorney general to make agreements with state and local governments permitting them to enforce immigration laws; as of October 2002 only Florida had concluded such an agreement. However, the Justice Department drafted an opinion in 2002 arguing that state and local law enforcement already have "inherent authority" to make arrests for civil immigration violations. The memo, seen as signaling an important shift, sparked strong opposition from civil liberties organizations and from many local police forces, and has not yet been issued publicly. *See* James M. Lindsay and Audrey Singer, "Local Police Should Not Do a Federal Job," *New York Times,* May 8, 2002; Darryl Fears, "Hispanic Group Assails INS Enforcement Plan," *Washington Post,* July 23, 2002; and Migration Policy Institute, "Authority of State and Local Officers to Arrest Aliens Suspected of Civil Infractions of Federal Immigration Law," June 11, 2002, <www.migration policy.org> (Oct. 25, 2002).

window and not stay focused on the criminal justice system and the Constitution.[4]

James Ashton
Virginia Department of Education (representing Dr. Jo Lynne DeMary, state superintendent of public instruction, Virginia Department of Education)

Our response to September 11 drew on crisis management systems that the Virginia Department of Education had put in place and that school divisions had been perfecting for the last three or four years. These systems allowed us to possibly avert some problems that could have occurred. The vast majority of school divisions in the state provided counseling to students and parents to help them cope with the events of September 11. Some offered special counseling to Muslim children and to all directly affected children. In at least four or five school divisions, Muslim imams in the area came in to assist.

Many positive changes have occurred in schools since September 11, which have resulted in the formation of new partnerships and networks. Many PTAs have held international awareness days to promote tolerance of cultural and religious differences. Also, the Farmville, Virginia, community held an interdenominational religious ceremony. Many organizations assisted schools in planning special activities, especially in Northern Virginia and the Tidewater area where there are many ethnic groups. The Virginia Association of Multicultural Educators conference will feature a dialogue with representatives of groups affected by September 11, including Muslims and Sikhs.[5]

Brian Boykins
Assistant district commander, Mason District, Fairfax County Police, Virginia

Prior to September 11, we had established the Bias Incident Unit to improve the reporting of hate incidents, and we reached out to diverse communities to hear their concerns. Shortly after the terrorist attacks, we put out public messages that hate crimes would not be tolerated and violators would be prosecuted. Unfortu-

nately, since September 11 we've seen an increase in reported bias incidents, some of which is due to our change in reporting procedures.

As a black person in America I bring a unique perspective, as this whole scenario of hatred played out not too long ago in relation to African Americans. Now we're right back here dealing with hatred again. I'm proud that I can go into a variety of communities and make clear that this type of behavior is unacceptable and will not be tolerated.

As far as racial profiling being used to identify potential terrorists, in law enforcement we should be focusing on behavior rather than on racial and ethnic stereotypes that are insignificant. For example, several of the terrorists went to flight school and only wanted to learn how to take off, not how to land. That should have been a red flag, regardless of their race or ethnicity.[6]

Penelope Gross
Member of the board of directors, Metropolitan Washington Council of Governments, and Mason District supervisor, Fairfax County, Virginia

On September 11, the emergency response at the Pentagon was rapid and highly professional. Where the Council of Governments saw gaps was in other areas, away from the Pentagon. As a result, we have been working hard for months to develop a regional emergency coordination plan so the region can be better prepared should another emergency occur.

Although much of it deals with technical aspects, emergency planning also needs to include a cultural component. When the September 11 attacks hit, certain members of our community were suddenly seen in a different way. In an emergency, our first responders always have to keep in mind that everyone must be treated with dignity and respect.

Wearing my hat as Mason District supervisor, I would like to emphasize that our local response here in Mason District started long before September 11. The population of the district includes longtime residents who've been here since the 1940s as well as many new immigrants, and frictions were apparent. In 1998 I developed a group called Kaleidoscope, which

---

[4] Summary of testimony by Charles Moose, Forum Transcript, pp. 425–29, 481–90, 507–10, 519–22.

[5] Summary of testimony by James Ashton, Forum Transcript, pp. 429–35, 501–02, 518.

[6] Summary of testimony by Brian Boykins, Forum Transcript, pp. 436–41, 478–79, 488–89, 510.

meets once a month and has held two town meetings to talk about cultural issues in the community and build greater understanding. Kaleidoscope has established networking and socializing among people who never would have met one another otherwise.

This good will was tested on September 11. That afternoon, five Muslim clerics came to my office expressing their great fear of a backlash that would put women and children in danger. At my suggestion, they held a multicultural prayer service at the Dar Al-Hijra mosque involving local ministers, members of the school board, and the community. This effort drew on the relationships we had begun building at least two years before.

The fallout from September 11 affected all immigrants in this country, not only Arabs and South Asians. It affected them psychologically, making them feel as if they're moving backward in the process of acceptance. For example, there was a tremendous impact on the Latino community.[7]

Sharee Freeman
Director, Community Relations Service,
Department of Justice

The District of Columbia, Maryland, and Virginia have done a super job of dealing with the aftermath of September 11.

After the terrorist attacks, the attorney general made a public service announcement condemning hate crimes, and we told our U.S. attorneys throughout the country to make similar statements. In the months since then, the Community Relations Service of DOJ has undertaken intensive outreach throughout the nation. We are:

- Ensuring state and local responses to hate incidents.

- Responding directly to situations of ethnic or racial conflict.

- Setting up resolution teams to help state and local officials.

- Doing outreach to Arab American, Muslim, and Sikh organizations to offer them assistance in resolving reported hate crime and incidents, and to promote dialogue between them and local authorities.

- Working with school officials to reduce school and campus tensions.

- Building cooperation among federal agencies.

- Working with interfaith alliances.

- Working with organizers of protest marches, notably Palestinians and Israelis, to prevent violence at these events.

The raids in Northern Virginia in March were done by the law enforcement side of the Treasury Department. CRS has stayed away from that issue. CRS is not a law enforcement agency. We did have several meetings with some national groups on the subject, but we have not engaged in any community activities focusing on this.

As regards the discussion of local police doing immigration enforcement, at present there has to be a memorandum of agreement between the Justice Department and a local police force before this type of activity can take place. That has only happened in one state. I think we all recognize that it's a new day. And it may surprise you to know that some Muslim communities outside the Beltway have been telling us, go get these bad guys and do whatever it takes. I think having community forums like this is one way to help achieve balance in our policies, with respect to making sure that what happened on September 11 never happens again.[8]

Susan Douglas
Principal researcher, Council on Islamic Education

Efforts to build understanding between Muslims and non-Muslims didn't start on September 11, 2001. We've long known that we need to teach American students about other cultures and religions, about geography and history, about where the United States fits into the world. The Council on Islamic Education has co-published a study that explains state requirements in curriculum about religion in a way that

---

[7] Summary of testimony by Penelope Gross, Forum Transcript, pp. 441–52, 480–81, 490–91, 498–501, 504–05, 508–09, 512–13, 516–17.

[8] Summary of testimony by Sharee Freeman, Forum Transcript, pp. 452–60, 477–80, 484, 491–93, 497–98, 522–23.

fits within a constitutional framework, and we have also prepared materials for teaching about Islam and Muslims in the public schools.[9]

Educational efforts on these themes have greatly accelerated since September 11. State departments of education across the country responded within hours of the attacks to help schools deal with the event and avoid hate. There has been a flurry of teacher training workshops and presentations over the last eight months.

Fairfax County Public Schools has a proactive approach that involves dual efforts for enhancing community outreach and social studies standards to include broader teachings about the world. They set up an Arab and Muslim task force of community members and educators that held a number of meetings in the fall of 2001 to address the responses of the schools in preventing hate violence.

The structures for teaching tolerance are in place, and we need to continue to do more of the same.[10]

Jason Erb
Government relations officer, Council on American-Islamic Relations

The initial local response to the backlash was good around the country. Police provided protection to mosques to prevent vandalism and hate crimes. Local officials did outreach and made public statements urging people not to turn on their neighbors. There were numerous prayer vigils and other public events.

Many Muslim immigrants in this country are somewhat isolated from the larger community, so in times of crisis, they're out of touch with local officials. However, that was not necessarily the case here in Virginia and Maryland, where the Muslim communities are so large. Efforts to build good relations between Muslims and non-Muslims in the area began well before September 11 and will continue.

Nonetheless, there is a continuing stream of hate language, for example, on local radio talk shows. Commentators make statements about Islam that show their ignorance, and these statements are not being challenged as much now as they were in the immediate aftermath of September 11. And given the involvement of the United States in various crises around the world, we will probably see the backlash against Muslims spike again, increasing their alienation from the larger society. We need to remain vigilant and work to prevent that.

There have been cases in parts of the country where the local response was not appropriate, where local police rounded up immigrants for no real reason. Furthermore, the federal government is now talking about using local law enforcement to help enforce immigration policies. When people are stopped for a traffic violation and then asked about their immigration status, this undermines the community's trust. A number of police forces actually refused to cooperate with the "voluntary" interviews of 5,000 Arab and Muslim men because they knew it would destroy trust. On the other hand, in some other places local law enforcement was eager to round up and expel Muslims. Most of the 1,200 people detained after September 11 were held on very minor visa violations, and in the voluntary interviews, immigration questions topped the list. Those interviews have led in some cases to weeks and months of detention without charges. This has sent the wrong message to the community.

The September 11 tragedy has provided an opportunity for Muslim and non-Muslim communities in the United States to work together toward greater mutual understanding and recognize some of the stereotypes on both sides. We need to continue these efforts given the likelihood that other events will again raise tensions within the community.[11]

---

[9] Council on Islamic Education, *Teaching About Islam and Muslims in the Public School Classroom,* <http://www.aaiusa.org/educational_packet.htm> (Oct. 28, 2002).

[10] Summary of testimony by Susan Douglas, Forum Transcript, pp. 460–70, 518–19.

[11] Summary of testimony by Jason Erb, Forum Transcript, 470–76, 494–96, 511–12.

Chapter 8

Key Observations Based on Forum Testimony

In July 2002, the U.S. Commission on Civil Rights strongly reiterated its commitment to protecting the rights of vulnerable groups in the post-September 11 environment, affirming that:

> combating terrorism should never become a war against Arab Americans or Muslims, or any group based on religion or national origin. . . . Maintaining a secure homeland does not justify discrimination against Arab Americans and others today, any more than World War II justified the internment of innocent Japanese Americans over a half century ago.[1]

The April 2002 forum in Annandale, Virginia, conducted as a joint project by the District of Columbia, Maryland, and Virginia Advisory Committees provided a wealth of information on the post-September 11 backlash and on threats to civil liberties related to the government's war on terrorism. The forum also called attention to positive efforts to prevent hate violence and discrimination and to increase dialogue and understanding between members of the affected communities and others.

Based on the testimony at the forum, the Inter-SAC Committee offers three broad observations about the way forward.

Observation 1:

Hate violence and discrimination have had a severe impact on people of Arab, South Asian, Muslim, and Sikh backgrounds in the Washington, D.C., metropolitan area, and across the United States, in the wake of the September 11, 2001, terrorist attacks.

These groups, which are solidly part of American society, publicly condemned the September 11 attacks and want to see the perpetrators brought to justice. Nonetheless, over the past year persons of Arab, South Asian, Muslim, and Sikh backgrounds, as well as others mistaken for members of these communities, have been made scapegoats and subjected to intense hate violence, harassment, and discrimination in various arenas of public life.

The hundreds of hate incidents documented across the country in the weeks and months following September 11 have included murder, attempted murder, assault, death threats, and hate speech against individuals, as well as vandalism, arson, and threats against homes, schools, businesses, and places of worship. Individuals wearing distinctive dress, that is, Muslim women and Sikhs, appear to have been singled out frequently for attacks. Like most parts of the country, the Washington, D.C., metropolitan area saw an increase in reported hate incidents. However, immediately after the hijackings local authorities began proactive outreach to vulnerable groups and took steps to protect them, such as by stationing police cruisers outside mosques. These efforts continued for some weeks afterward and may have helped to prevent more serious injuries in the Washington, D.C., metropolitan area.

While reported hate incidents have tapered off gradually since September 2001, the Inter-SAC Committee takes very seriously the continuing threat of violence against innocent people who are in no way to blame for the terrorist atrocities and who, in a sense, form a second set of victims of the September 11 attacks. The U.S. war in Iraq has raised new concerns about the

[1] U.S. Commission on Civil Rights, "Civil Rights Commission Reaffirms Commitment to Protecting Rights of Arab Americans and Muslims," press release, July 24, 2002.

possibility of a renewed surge of discrimination and violence against people of Middle Eastern background in the United States. Local law enforcement should be vigilant in identifying and promptly prosecuting alleged perpetrators of hate violence, and should continue working with the affected communities and interested organizations to track and prosecute violations. Where appropriate, charges should also be brought under federal hate crime statutes.

Discrimination against people who appear to be Arab, South Asian, Muslim, or Sikh is proving to be a persistent problem as well, particularly in the workplace and in air travel. Panelists reported that ethnic, national, and religious discrimination is rampant within the nation's air travel system, even though federal agencies have advised the airlines that it is illegal. Of particular concern are cases in which travelers have been denied boarding or removed from aircraft after having passed through security screening, or have been required to remove religiously mandated head coverings for no legitimate reason. Mechanisms are in place for members of the public to file complaints about airline discrimination, and representatives of federal agencies said at the forum that these complaints are investigated thoroughly. But it is not clear that the process of filing complaints is doing much to prevent new instances of discrimination in the absence of standardized and consistently enforced security policies, procedures, and training for airline personnel.

In responding to the backlash, the federal government appears to be playing an inconsistent role that contains both positive and negative elements. The U.S. Justice Department's Civil Rights Division has publicly warned against hate violence and discrimination, created a special post-September 11 initiative, reached out to vulnerable communities, and opened 350 investigations into alleged hate crimes as well as numerous civil investigations into noncriminal bias incidents. The department's Community Relations Service has been working with communities across the country on state and local responses to hate incidents. The Equal Employment Opportunity Commission was commended for its responsiveness to complaints of workplace discrimination.

At the same time, several panelists representing affected communities reported that official statements of concern by high-ranking federal officials and receptiveness to complaints by various government agencies frequently are not followed up with action. Furthermore, the federal government has sent contradictory messages through its actions. While some officials are verbally cautioning Americans not to engage in ethnic or religious discrimination, other federal authorities are actively making use of ethnic and religious profiling as they round up members of these communities for questioning, detention, and deportation. When federal agents knock down doors of Arab American homes and handcuff the residents, or select people for interrogation apparently based on their ethnic or religious background, and without adequate public explanation, these actions have a negative impact on our country. They send a strong message to members of the public that their Arab, South Asian, Muslim, and Sikh neighbors are likely to be guilty of something—even if the government never says what. This contributes to an environment in which members of the public feel free to act on whatever feelings of fear, anger, and hate they may harbor.

Observation 2:

Tactics currently being used to pursue the federal government's war on terrorism pose a threat to civil liberties, and history gives reason to doubt their potential effectiveness. The government can and should pursue an effective antiterrorism strategy that fully respects the Constitution.

A theme running through the forum presentations was that "history repeats itself." Panelists noted that the current roundups, detentions, and deportations of foreign-born persons under conditions of secrecy and without access to legal counsel recall some of the most shameful episodes in U.S. history, including the Palmer raids in 1919 and the detention of Japanese Americans during World War II. They further observed that many of the tactics being used in the government's antiterrorism efforts, such as the attempt to establish guilt based on association and use of secret evidence, were also used in past investigations such as COINTELPRO in the 1960s. After the domestic spying abuses of the 1960s and 1970s, a series of rules and constraints was imposed to limit the government's power over citizens; but since September 11 many of these checks and balances have been eliminated or suspended, with worrisome implications for civil liberties.

The USA Patriot Act gives the government sweeping new enforcement powers with far-reaching implications. These new powers are being applied without meaningful judicial review. They apply to all federal investigations, not only those related to terrorism, and they have been used to conduct interrogations and to raid homes of U.S. citizens and other legal residents without allowing them access to normal legal protections. Thus these serious threats to civil liberties affect the whole nation.

Panelists identified two major problems with the tactics being used. First, they are likely to be ineffective.[2] Ethnic and religious profiling, reliance on guilt by association and secret evidence, and exemption of government actions from oversight and accountability have failed in the past to detect actual criminal activity and are likely to prove just as unreliable in the current context. To the extent that government investigators target people based on their ethnic or religious background, these actions are at best inefficient and ineffective protection against terrorism. Profiling by ethnic or religious identity casts too wide a net and does not focus on persons actually engaged in provable criminal activity. Shielding government activity from view and relying on secret evidence run the risk of wasting government resources building empty cases against the wrong individuals.

Second, these tactics are alienating communities whose help the government has said it wants. The federal government has asked Arabs and Muslims in the United States to assist in identifying potential sources of terrorist activity, but at the same time it is angering and intimidating those communities through aggressive violations of their civil rights. Racial profiling, searches, interrogations, detentions, deportations, and violent raids on homes and businesses have led to deep distrust of the authorities among members of the communities targeted. People may want to help the antiterrorism effort with information, but they are hardly likely to

come forward if by doing so they risk being detained or deported.

The government must have the powers it needs to ensure the nation's security, but history shows that we cannot purchase national security by giving up our civil liberties. The government can and must devise an effective antiterrorism strategy that respects the Constitution—by focusing on criminal activity rather than guilt by association; by ensuring judicial review and control; by requiring accountability for results; and by ensuring oversight by Congress, the Justice Department, and outside organizations.

Observation 3:

Efforts are urgently needed to increase the U.S. public's understanding of Arabs, South Asians, Muslims, and Sikhs, and to promote dialogue between people of different religious and ethnic backgrounds.

Organizations representing Arab Americans and other affected groups have long been concerned about the public's general lack of knowledge about their communities and the prevalence of negative stereotypes. The events of September 11 reinforced the most damaging stereotypes about Arabs and Muslims, setting the stage for hate violence against them and others perceived to resemble them, especially Sikhs. Panelists stressed the urgency of countering this ignorance with education and dialogue, and noted that the tragic events of September 11 have created new opportunities for such efforts.

The Muslim imams, scholars, and advocates who addressed the forum emphasized that Islam is a religion based on concepts of peace, justice, and equity, and has much in common with Christianity and Judaism; the faith condemns suicide and homicide and the killing of unarmed civilians. They stressed that Muslims in the United States overwhelmingly condemned the horrific terrorist acts and reject the notion that these acts are religiously justified by Islam or reflect on the nature of the faith. The panelists examined and debunked key stereotypes, such as the notion that Islam is incompatible with democracy.

In the Washington, D.C., metropolitan area, efforts to promote understanding between different ethnic and religious groups began well before September 11, 2001, and these efforts provided a firm foundation for the post-September 11 response. Of particular note are programs in

---

[2] As noted in chapter 5, the Inter-SAC Committee invited the Department of Justice to send a representative who could address the department's antiterrorism policies and procedures regarding their appropriateness and effectiveness. However, the office charged with communicating department policies to the public declined the invitation to participate. (*See* footnote 4, page 20).

schools to promote understanding among different groups of students and parents, as well as interfaith programs and secular community-based programs. The Committee members heard about an initiative called Kaleidoscope, which brings together the diverse populations of Mason District in Fairfax County, Virginia, and which could serve as a model for other communities. In the months since the attacks, additional programs have been initiated in school systems and communities around Washington, D.C., aimed at bringing people together and building understanding and tolerance.

Nonetheless, communities, schools, and religious bodies must do more, by redoubling their support for successful programs and creating new initiatives modeled on best practices. A recurring theme of the backlash is the targeting of violence and discrimination against individuals whose dress is distinctive, especially those who wear head coverings—the *hijabs* worn by some Muslim women and the turbans worn by nearly all observant Sikhs. These articles of clothing appear to have become, in the minds of some Americans, symbols of foreignness, of "otherness," even of terrorism and sympathy for Osama bin Laden. At the most basic level, therefore, steps should be taken to educate the public about the meaning of religiously mandated clothing and hairstyles in a variety of faiths. Beyond that, communities have much work to do in the difficult but critically important task of teaching tolerance and respect for differences in religion, language, culture, and appearance that are so much a part of American society today.

Appendix 1

Dissenting Statement by Stephen Kurzman, DC SAC Member

Re: Inter-SAC Report on September 11 Aftermath

I cannot in good conscience sign the proposed report in its present form, because it is seriously unbalanced. In the "Observations" section the report simply adopts the broadest, most critical conclusions of the non-governmental witnesses, without any analysis of the difficult balancing required between national security and civil liberties in particular, different types of cases (for example, distinguishing between temporary visitors, permanent residents, citizens, and enemy combatants) or of the remedies that are available to those who are aggrieved (such as habeas corpus, criminal complaints, unlawful arrest suits, or suits to quash search warrants).

The report dismisses in one sentence here and there the repeated, extensive, and widely publicized efforts by government officials, from the President of the United States on down, to prevent violence, harassment or discrimination against the affected communities and individuals. The report also peremptorily dismisses the testimony of the government witnesses at the forum and ignores the enormous domestic security challenge facing federal, state and local governments and all inhabitants of the U.S.

The forum itself had the same unreal quality. For example, there was repeated testimony protesting against the March, 2002, raid by U.S. Treasury agents in Northern Virginia on businesses, non-profit organizations, and four homes, all apparently related to one person, but no mention of the fact that the raid was conducted under court-ordered search warrants accusing the respondents of funding terrorist groups. There was reference to a meeting with the Secretary of the Treasury to protest the raid and disappointment with the lack of follow-up but no reference to legal action available if the raid was unjustified.

Similarly, criticism of reporting requirements for temporary visitors from certain countries as "ethnic profiling" is not balanced by recognition of the problem posed by entry under temporary visitor visas, and subsequent violations of the terms of those visas, of individuals who have and would harm us, particularly from countries that have been listed as sponsoring terrorism or harboring terrorists. Yet the report highlights testimony on topics, such as U.S. policy toward the Middle East and the alleged motivations of radical Islamist terrorists, which are irrelevant to the subject the witnesses were asked to address.

Nor does the report reflect the relevant court decisions and indictments during the nine months since the forum. Consideration of these developments might have moderated the report's suggestion that the anti-terrorism tactics so far employed are unconstitutional and ineffective and will inevitably lead to a repeat of the World War II internment of Japanese-American citizens or the other deplorable, crisis-era civil liberty lapses in our nation's history. It already appears that this time the courts are not reflexively coming down on the national security side but are looking closely at each case and trying to achieve a proper balance.

The USCCR and its SAC's, along with non-governmental groups and individuals, could play a useful role in speaking up for civil rights and civil liberties in specific, questionable cases. For example, challenges are being litigated currently about the constitutionality of denying counsel and court review to U.S. citizens declared to be enemy combatants and whether it matters that they have been captured on a foreign battlefield or in the U.S. But in discussing these and other tactics against terrorism within the constraints of the law and the Constitution, thoughtful analysis of the particulars and balancing of the competing goals are required. Sweeping generalizations, on either side of these difficult issues, do not, in my judgment, advance the debate.

Finally, the draft report, like the forum on which it is based, is fundamentally flawed because of its overly-ambitious scope. SAC's across the country were asked by the Commission to investigate what happened to the affected populations in their jurisdictions following September 11, 2001, and what the relevant government bodies did to respond. Our Inter-SAC Committee could have provided a useful body of data if we had confined ourselves to that important subject. But, even though we represent only three jurisdictions, our committee instead went far beyond that charge, trying to educate the American public about the religion of Islam, an enormous and complex subject in itself, and to cover post-September 11 impacts on the affected populations throughout the country, all in a day and a half of testimony. The unfortunate result is that, except for one useful piece of testimony on the demographics of the Washington metropolitan area and the incomplete references to the Northern Virginia raid, the record is very slim about our area of the country. As a result, what happened in our three jurisdictions affecting civil rights and civil liberties and what the various government agencies have done here is, sadly, not apparent in the draft report.

Stephen Kurzman

January 25, 2003

Appendix 2

Editorial Committee's Clarifications to the Dissenting Statement by Stephen Kurzman

After reviewing the opinion written by the colleague who cast the solitary dissent in the 37 to 1 vote, the Inter-SAC Editorial Committee concluded that unless supplemented by clarifying information, the dissenting opinion misrepresents and thereby likely undermines the report. Therefore, the Editorial Committee, consisting of six members—the chairperson and one member each from the District of Columbia, Maryland, and Virginia Advisory Committees (SACs)—decided to issue a joint statement of how it went about planning and implementing its April 2002 forum and what its purposes were to place the dissention in context. This statement of clarifications first describes the procedures and decision-making process followed throughout the project and then comments on five substantive points.

1. Process

In early November 2002 the three SACs in the Washington metropolitan area decided to undertake a joint inter-SAC project on civil rights issues in the aftermath of the 9/11 attacks and formed the 9/11 Inter-SAC Committee. Its first step was to form the Inter-SAC Planning Committee, consisting of the chairperson and an additional three members from each SAC, charging it with the responsibilities of planning a community forum on behalf of the three participating SACs and also soliciting input from other members. The final plan for the forum, developed and adopted step-by-step by the Planning Committee, was shared with all members of the three participating SACs to ensure that the plans reflected as diverse viewpoints as possible. This plan included five issue-specific panels and identified advocates, community representatives, and federal, state, and local agencies that would be invited to participate.

In order to maximize SAC involvement in the forum, all members of the three participating SACs were invited to sit on as many panels as they wished. The Planning Committee also designated one member from these volunteers to serve as the panel moderator. Each panel subcommittee, consisting of a moderator and volunteer members, prepared questions and issues for invited panelists to address.

As the project progressed to the report-drafting stage, the Inter-SAC Editorial Committee was formed to serve as the collective editor with attendant prerogatives. Although the Editorial Committee was small, every effort was made to ensure maximum input from all members of the three SACs, by sharing three draft versions of the report and each time soliciting input.

Mr. Kurzman served on both the Planning Committee and the subcommittee for the "Understanding Islam in America in the Aftermath of 9/11" panel. Every SAC member was given ample opportunity and urged to participate in decisionmaking regarding project planning and report drafting, although at times decisions were made by majority rule when consensus was not possible.

2. Scope

The Planning Committee considered whether the project should limit its focus to local issues or provide a wider perspective and a context to help the SAC members, forum attendees, and readers of the resulting report. Opinions varied, with some arguing that the forum should go as far and deep as looking into the root causes of anti-Arab, anti-Muslim, and anti-American sentiment, while others preferred to remain focused on local issues. After lengthy debate, the Planning Committee ultimately decided by majority vote to include three background panels, "Understanding Islam in America in the Aftermath of 9/11," "National Crises, Civil Rights Protections, and Civil Liberties: A Historical Review," and "Implementing the USA Patriot Act of 2001: Civil Rights Impact." These panels were intended to provide background information to help better understand the civil rights issues discussed at the forum. The wide scope of the project was a deliberate decision of the Planning Committee.

3. Mission of the Advisory Committees and the purpose of the forum

The Planning Committee recognizes that government agencies and law enforcement officials face a delicate task of attending to national security concerns while providing due civil rights protections. It becomes more difficult when national security is violated or continually threatened. However, the responsibility of the SACs is to highlight civil rights concerns and issues where they exist. It is beyond the mandate of the SACs, and the scope of this project, to enter into lengthy discussions of the difficulties involved in protecting national security while respecting the civil rights of its population. Neither was it the intent of the forum to be a critical arbiter of the citizen complaints or to be an apologist for the actions of federal government agencies. Consistent with the idea of serving as the "ears and eyes" for the Commission, the purpose of the forum was to gather information on the fears and concerns of minority communities affected by the 9/11 attacks and public officials' responses to the concerns expressed and their preventive or ameliorative actions.

4. Efforts by government agencies

The Planning Committee made extensive efforts to learn of and report on the actions taken by federal and local government agencies to prevent violence, harassment, discrimination, and other civil rights violations of the affected communities in the District of Columbia, Maryland, and Virginia. A total of 13 public officials (seven federal and six local government officials) were invited to participate in the forum to ensure that these preventive measures were fairly conveyed to the public. However, several of the invited government and elected officials (two federal and one local official) did not attend the forum.

The representatives of the federal government who were present provided the Inter-SAC Committee with a wealth of information. For example, two representatives from the U.S. Department of Justice (DOJ) discussed the department's investigation of civil rights abuses by both DOJ employees and private individuals against Arabs, persons of Islamic and Sikh faiths, and those perceived to be of Middle Eastern descent. The representative from DOJ's Community Relations Service described the department's efforts not only to convey directly its concerns for civil rights to affected communities, but also to assist victims of harassment and violence. In addition, public officials from local governments (including police chiefs and administrators) from Maryland and Virginia discussed their collaborative work with federal agencies to investigate threats of terrorism, pursue terrorist suspects, and protect civil rights and liberties. Two representatives from the U.S. Department of Transportation also discussed the department's efforts for civil rights protections for persons traveling by air in the United States within the context of domestic security challenges, describing both the system by which persons are identified as possible threats and safeguards the government uses to prevent discrimination.

5. Post-forum developments

The report is a summary of panel presentations that took place in April 2002. The information contained in the report results from the testimony of those panelists that the members of the District of Columbia, Maryland, and Virginia SACs chose to invite to the forum. The report highlights individual testimonies received, and reflects the views and opinions of the panelists who attended. The Planning Committee never intended to go beyond this limited goal. As much as it might be useful to compile major post-9/11 court decisions and provide a pertinent legal analysis, to do so is neither the purpose of the report nor within its intended scope.

This Inter-SAC report is only one component of the Commission's work on post-9/11 civil rights issues; other SACs have held fact-finding briefings both before and after the April 2002 forum. The Commission continues to report on the various developments concerning post-9/11 civil rights concerns.

6. Reference to the raids in Northern Virginia

An appropriate footnote has been added in chapter 3 of the report to indicate that U.S. Treasury agents conducted the raids under search warrants. It also provides a description from news accounts of the raids and their psychological impact on one family subjected to a raid. More germane to the report, however, is the fact that the repeated references by panelists to the U.S. Treasury agents' raids underscore how large the event looms in the minds of the Muslim community, whether or not the raids occurred with valid search warrants.

Editorial Committee
Lewis Anthony
Sheila Carter-Tod
Cynthia Graae
Debra Lemke
Richard Patrick
Chester Wickwire

May 1, 2003